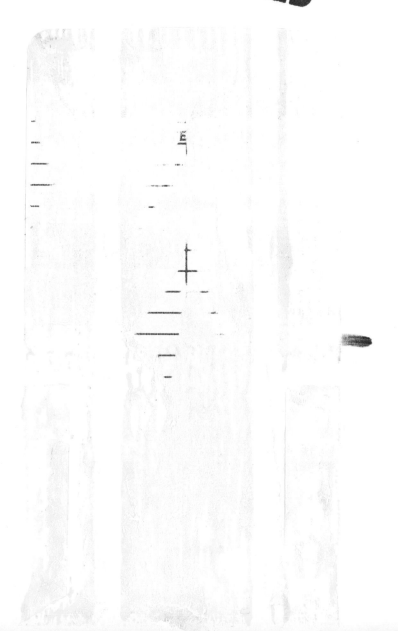

PSYCHOLOGY AND CHRISTIANITY

An Introduction to Controversial Issues

Ronald P. Philipchalk

UNIVERSITY
PRESS OF
AMERICA

Lanham • New York • London

Copyright © 1987 by

University Press of America,® Inc.

4720 Boston Way
Lanham, MD 20706

3 Henrietta Street
London WC2E 8LU England

British Cataloging in Publication Information Available

Library of Congress Cataloging-in-Publication Data

Philipchalk, Ronald P., 1945-
  Psychology and Christianity.

  Includes bibliographies and indexes.
  1. Psychology and religion. 2. Christianity—
Psychology. I. Title.
BF51.P48   1987   261.5'15   87-15971
ISBN 0-8191-6537-9 (alk. paper)
ISBN 0-8191-6538-7 (pbk. : alk. paper)

All University Press of America books are produced on acid-free
paper which exceeds the minimum standards set by the National
Historical Publication and Records Commission.

To my parents, who taught
me early the importance of
truth.

CONTENTS

Chapter 3
SENSATION AND PERCEPTION...45

> Should Christians use conditioning techniques?

PREFACE

"Don't take 'Psychology'--they teach you about yourself and it takes all the fun away."

Whether or not it takes all the fun away, as this student warned, millions of people study psychology every year in order to learn about themselves. Since its humble beginnings approximately a century ago, psychology has grown to be one of the most popular fields of study in North America today. Year after year more college students choose to take courses in psychology than in any other area. Books on psychology and psychological problems abound, frequently topping the best seller lists.

Christians too are fascinated by psychology. However, their fascination is often tinged by a good deal of fear, for they are suspicious of this human enterprise which attempts to explain (and even explain away) in cold scientific terms, their most intimate spiritual workings. Nowhere is this more obvious than in the many Introductory Psychology classes which I have taught. Year after year I find the same questions being raised both in class and out as students struggle to relate psychological phenomena to their Christian values and experiences.

Good books and articles exist on the theoretical level of "the integration of psychology and Christianity"; good work has been done at the practical level of Christian therapy. However, most of these do not deal with the questions my students (and I assume others) raise: "Could religious experience have a physical basis?" "Is ESP harmful?" "Can Christians use hypnosis?" "Should I love myself or hate myself?" Christianity and psychology need to be brought together at this often difficult, "thorny" level too.

This book is written in an attempt to both facilitate and further stimulate this process. It attempts to "illustrate" an approach to issues with which Christians frequently struggle. Although this approach is based upon Biblical assumptions which recognize the fundamental reliability of Divine revelation, it does not mean that we

xiii

approach the issues with blinders on.   As C.S. Lewis said,

> ...I do not of course mean any attempt to make our intellectual enquiries work out to edifying conclusions.   That would be, as Bacon says, to offer to the author of truth the unclean sacrifice of a lie. I mean the pursuit of knowledge and beauty, in a sense, for their own sake, but in a sense which does not exclude their being for God's sake. ([1949] 1984, p.33).

Specifically our purpose is three-fold:

1. To put each of the sub-areas of psychology into perspective from a Christian point of view.

2. To anticipate questions frequently raised by Christians (and thrown at Christians) and to give some tentative answers.

3. To raise further questions and so to stimulate further thought.

The organization of the book is into 10 chapters plus a Conclusion.   Each chapter deals with a traditional sub-area within psychology.   Each chapter begins with a brief overview of the subject area (e.g., perception, psychotherapy, etc.) suggesting the relationship of this area to Christianity and a biblical view of man. Next, one or two issues which have proven controversial, particularly from a conservative Christian perspective, are presented. Significant questions are raised and tentative solutions suggested although frequently the reader is left to decide between alternative solutions, each of which has been found acceptable by different Christians.   The primary goal is to stimulate thought and discussion so that the reader may work through his own position and not be "spoon-fed" one proclaimed as "the Christian position."

Each chapter ends with provocative further questions for thought and discussion.   These may be suitable for small group interaction or essay topics in an academic setting.   Each chapter contains a briefly annotated "Suggested Readings" section as well as a substantial list of "References and Other Sources."

The division into the sub-areas chosen follows that used by most textbooks of Introductory Psychology. In this way this book may be used as a companion to a standard textbook of Introductory Psychology, stimulating thought and discussion. Students may be asked to evaluate the positions presented, or to take a side on one of the "further issues", using the bibliography provided for further research.

For those who do not have a textbook handy, the introductory section of each chapter will supply the context for the later discussion. Many of the bibliographic materials are popular books and articles available in most church libraries or Christian book stores.

It is hoped that this book will provide a helpful guide to Christians interested in psychology whether as formal students (past or present) or as informal enquirers seeking to remain in touch with critical issues in the interface between psychology and Christianity. It is my conviction that every Christian has something to contribute to the development of Christian psychology. May this book in some small way, be a catalyst in this important process.

CHAPTER 1: PSYCHOLOGY AND CHRISTIANITY

THE STUDY OF MIND AND BEHAVIOR
EVERYDAY KNOWLEDGE
PSYCHOLOGY EVERYWHERE
CONTROVERSIAL ISSUES

> 1. How can psychology and Christianity be related?
> 2. Is there a "school of Christian psychology?"

The lines drawn.
RELATING PSYCHOLOGY AND CHRISTIANITY
    Psychology is suspect.
    Psychology is trustworthy.
    Viewpoint.
    Levels of explanation.
    Summary.
CHRISTIAN PSYCHOLOGY TODAY
SCHOOLS OF PSYCHOLOGY
A CHRISTIAN SCHOOL OF PSYCHOLOGY?
DISCUSSION QUESTIONS
    Scientific method.
    Christian psychology.
    Christian school of psychology.
SUGGESTED READINGS
REFERENCES AND OTHER SOURCES

"Psychology is...
   rats running mazes,
   pigeons pecking keys,
   a neurotic on a couch,
   electrodes in the brain,
   multiple-choice tests,
   deceptive experiments,
   ink-blot stories,
   I.Q. tests,
          ...that's what psychology is."

What have all these impressions in common? They are all part of an attempt to understand ourselves. Humans have always wondered about themselves; from the psalmist's "What is man that Thou art mindful of him?" to the contemporary "search for identity." People have continually asked themselves such questions as "Why do I act as I do?," "What is the meaning of my dreams?" "Why are people different from each other?". Historically such questions were considered primarily by philosophers. However, with the rapid development of science in the past two hundred years most of these questions have been taken over by the new "scientific philosophy" called psychology. Psychology may be seen as a new attempt, using principles of science, to answer some of man's oldest questions.

THE STUDY OF MIND AND BEHAVIOR

For centuries the study of humankind was the domain of philosophy and/or religion alone. With the development of scientific medicine and physiology, especially in the 19th century, some of the basic questions about human nature were brought into the laboratory. Here for example, the connection between the mind (or soul) and the body was subjected to intense scrutiny. Beginning with observations such as those by Fritsch and Hitzig, who roamed the battlefield in 1870 probing the exposed brains of dying soldiers with an electric current, the brain rapidly became, and continues to be, the focus of attention for the age-old "mind/body" question. Philosophy and physiology met in psychology.

When psychology began to develop in Europe as a unique discipline separate from physiology and

2

philosophy, about 125 years ago, it set as its task "the study of the mind." However, the concept of mind was found to be very elusive. Psychologists struggled with it for 50 or 60 years until an American named John Watson made the revolutionary proposal that since we can only study what we can observe and measure, and since we can't observe or measure minds, but only behavior, we will study behavior--and **only** behavior. The movement Watson began became known as "Behaviorism" and it dominated psychology for 50 years. It was during this time that animal studies became popular, largely through the influence of behaviorism's best known contemporary proponent, B.F. Skinner.

If you took courses in psychology in the 70s, or earlier, you would have found that psychology was defined in the textbooks of the day as "the scientific study of **behavior**." However, the narrowness of this approach has become increasingly obvious, primarily through the influence of humanist psychology. With its emphasis on the dignity, uniqueness, and potential of the person, humanist psychology has been an effective counterbalance to the narrowness of behaviorism. Today, introductory psychology textbooks define psychology as "the scientific study of behavior **and** mental processes" (or some such similar definition). Thus the pendulum has swung back to a more balanced position.

While psychology was developing in the labs and universities of Germany, Britain, and the U.S. at the end of the last century and the beginning of this, a separate development was taking place in the consulting rooms of a Viennese physician named Sigmund Freud--psychoanalysis was born. On the basis of his study and treatment of disturbed individuals Freud developed a very elaborate (some would say imaginative) theory of human behavior. While the psychoanalytic movement has never been fully incorporated into psychology (Schulz, 1981, p.339), it has nevertheless had a significant impact on psychology proper. Psychology owes to psychoanalysis the recognition of unconscious mental processes, defense mechanisms, and the importance of early childhood.

3

Contemporary psychology then, is a combination, an aggregate more than a blend, of physiology, philosophy, behaviorism, humanism, and psychoanalysis. From physiology psychology received its interest in the physical structures of the body, particularly, the brain, nervous system, and sense organs. From its philosophical roots psychology derived an interest in the mind/body problem, consciousness, and meaning. The movement called behaviorism has contributed an emphasis on scientific empiricism, experimentation, and measurement. The humanist movement has stressed a high view of humanity in its uniqueness. From psychoanalysis psychology has gained an appreciation for unconscious, instinctive and irrational sources of motivation. All of these have contributed to the diverse discipline which is contemporary North American psychology.

EVERYDAY KNOWLEDGE

As a behavioral science, psychology fits the description of all science attributed to Einstein-- "nothing more than the refinement of everyday knowledge." Whether this is knowledge of behavior or mental processes, psychology rarely does more than refine what was already known or at least frequently suspected. For example, everyday knowledge, or "folk wisdom," tells us that "opposites attract." Psychology will tell us some of the conditions under which this is true and when it is not. The bizarre and unusual findings sometimes associated with psychology often evaporate upon closer examination (e.g., "unconscious mind control"--Chapter 3) and we are left with "refined common sense."

This is not to say psychology is boring. It can be interesting and quite helpful to find out, for example, when it is "Never too old to learn" and when on the other hand "You can't teach an old dog new tricks." Moreover, research findings which may seem obvious are usually so only after they have been discovered. (This interesting psychological finding is called the "hindsight bias.")

4

PSYCHOLOGY EVERYWHERE

Finally, if you have not studied psychology you may be surprised to discover the range of interests psychologists have. A glance through the Table of Contents at the front of this book may have given you an inkling. And as we introduce various "controversial issues" some of psychology's breadth will become more apparent. Suffice it to say at this point that the popular notion of psychologists treating mental disorders encompasses but one aspect of the field. More than one third of the people with advanced degrees in psychology work in colleges and universities teaching and studying areas such as physiology, child development, human learning and memory, personality, testing, and social processes. A significant number of psychologists are also employed in other settings to train teachers, consult with industry, and design machines for human use. You may recall that psychology is defined as "the scientific study of behavior and mental processes"--a broad definition indeed. Although this study includes disorders, it is far from limited to them [1]

CONTROVERSIAL ISSUE

After this brief introduction to the field of psychology as a whole let us look at two related questions on the relationship between psychology and christianity:

---

1. How can psychology and Christianity be related?
2. Is there a "school of Christian psychology?"

---

1 For a more complete discussion of the fields of psychology consult any introductory text. Some possible sources are listed in the bibliography for this chapter.

In considering this first "controversial issue" we come face-to-face with one of the most basic and complex questions with which we have to deal. Is it possible to relate psychology and Christianity (other than as opponents)? And if so, how? A further, often implicit question, "Isn't contemporary psychology basically atheistic?" is also raised. To some people "Christian psychology" is a contradiction of terms. Is there any common ground for dialogue between psychology and Christianity?

In exploring this issue we will look first at the basis for the common antipathy between some Christians and psychology, and then examine some alternatives which different Christians have proposed for the relating of psychology and Christianity.

The lines drawn. Academics in general and psychologists in particular are among the least religious of all occupational groups.[1] Not only are they irreligious, they are frequently anti-religious. Psychologists have often taken a negative view of Christianity, rejecting it as something for "weak" individuals. Freud called it a neurosis, wish-fulfillment, and a carry-over from childhood dependence on the father. Ellis in a lecture on religion ("The case against religion," n.d.) said it is "... directly opposed to the goals of mental health...," Watson called it a "myth," and Maslow said it was "crap."[2] Others have been less blunt in their denunciation, choosing rather to ignore what they assume can be explained away psychologically.

On the other hand, many Christians have viewed psychology with distrust and even fear. Hearing the views of the psychologists noted above, one is not surprised to find some skepticism among Christians towards psychology. The fear that many Christians feel arises from several sources;

---

[1]. For a thorough review of the conflict between religion and psychology as well as psychoanalysis see Burnham (1985).

[2] .For further information on Ellis' view of religion see Saltzberg & Elkins (1980).

6

among these are (a) the suspicion that the secular
psychologists' criticisms may be right (as they
sometimes are), (b) the belief that a psychological
explanation "explains away" a spiritual one, and
(c) a failure to recognize all truth as God's (a
lesson we should have learned long ago from the
conflict of Galileo with the Church).

Psychology is so popular, and psychologists
treated with such deference in our society, that
their views can be extremely threatening to some
contemporary Christians. Let us examine some
ways Christians have dealt with this issue.

RELATING PSYCHOLOGY AND CHRISTIANITY

Various authors have proposed different systems
for categorizing approaches to relating psychology
and Christianity. This proliferation of terms can
produce confusion and reduce the effectiveness of
communication, as Hsieh (1982) has noted. Rather
than adopting one of these systems, or proposing a
new one, we will consider two broad viewpoints as
ends on a continuum. The continuum represents
the degree to which psychology as an independent
and unique discipline is accepted as a trustworthy
source of information for the understanding of
human behavior. [1]

Psychology is suspect. The simplest
approach for a cautious Christian to take in
relating psychology to Christianity is to reject
psychology outright. That is, psychology as a
discipline is rejected and its concerns are
subsumed under religion. This is the approach
taken by Jay Adams (1970, 1973), for example. [2]
Adams traces all problems to sin in the individual,
and sees in Scripture the answer to every

---

[1]. A conservative theological position, including the
reliability of Scripture, is assumed by the present
author and by those discussed here.

[2]. An outright rejection of psychology is also made by
D. Hunt and T. McMahon in their 1985 book "The
seduction of Christianity" (Irvine, CA: Harvest
House).

7

psychological problem. Recognizing the close relationship of spiritual and psychological problems, and observing that many psychologists do not take account of spiritual concerns, Adams moves in the other direction and treats all problems, except clearly organic ones, as purely spiritual--the individual needs to walk closer to God. From this point of view there is no useful psychology outside of a "Christian psychology," and no effective therapist who is not a Christian. Adams says, "The Bible does not need to be 'balanced' off by modern psychology. Nor may it be 'combined' with psychology to construct a balanced appoach" (1973, 92). This of course is not really "relating" psychology and Christianity but absorbing psychology into Christianity. Secular psychology as an independent discipline is rejected outright.

The general position from which this approach derives views psychology and Christianity as aliens which if they are to be related at all must be adapted to each other. Either Christians must reinterpret psychology, or psychology will reinterpret Christianity; either way a valuable perspective is lost. The underlying difficulty is a view of the world which sees natural and supernatural realms in inevitable and constant opposition. Less extreme "absorption" positions exist, but being based on the assumption that truth comes only or primarily through Scripture, they are prone to discount psychological findings which are inconsistent with their particular view of Scripture. God's revelation in creation,general revelation, is somehow not to be trusted and must always be reinterpreted to fit preconceived and immutable interpretations of Scripture. The trust placed in general revelation varies, and thus also does the amount of reinterpretation and the extent of "absorption" of psychology into Christianity.

Psychology is trustworthy. Towards the other end of our hypothetical continuum are those who value the insights of both psychology and Christianity. Although there are significant differences among them, they all place at least some trust in the findings of psychology (e.g., Collins, Ellens, Farnsworth, Koteskey, McLemore, Narramore). For these Christians the key to relating their disipline to Christianity lies in the assumption that God not only created the world but is actively involved in it. Thus, the study of God's creation and particularly the study of humans, is in part the study of God. God has revealed Himself most clearly in Jesus Christ. The Scriptures are the record of this and other specific revelation. But God is also revealing Himself in His ongoing creation as He brings His original work to fruition (natural revelation). Thus the study of humans, made in the image of God, is the study of not only His handiwork, but also His very likeness. And although this image is clouded in man's fallen state, it is still a resemblance which by the grace of God is capable of redemption and eventual restoration.

For these authors the task of relating theology or Christianity to psychology is not one of bringing together a discipline which points to God and one which does not. God is present in both, and the truths of either cannot conflict. To be sure interpretations may conflict.[1] When they do the intellectually honest task is to reinterpret, to change one, or the other, or both. The Christian's rejection of psychology is no better than the secular psychologist's rejection of Christianity. Both are examples of the same sort of intellectual narrowness.

The study of psychology is seen as the study of one work of a creating God (even a "co-creator" with God as Madeleine L'Engle (1983), so elegantly points out). Psychologists have the opportunity of not only studying His highest creation ("...a little lower than God," Ps. 8), but also in therapy participating with Him in that creation within the sphere of common grace. Whether it is helping to resolve a marriage problem, overcoming depression, or growing towards one's potential, giving this help is a Kingdom act, and a step towards the clarification of the image of God in another.

Viewpoint. Although our purpose in this book is to present issues for discussion and leave the

---

[1]. For a good discussion of the inevitability of psychological influences on interpretation see Johnson (1983).

9

reader to decide his or her own position, I cannot help revealing my own bias on this issue. If God "...made the heavens and the earth, the sea and all that is in them" (Ex. 20:11), and "upholds all things by the word of His power" (Heb. 1:3), and is "...in Christ reconciling the world to Himself" (II Cor. 5:19), then this creation, of which humans are a part, is worthy of study, especially if that study shows promise of aiding in the redemptive process. Certainly one must always avoid "...what is falsely called knowledge" (I Tim. 6:20), constantly affirming the reliability of Scripture (while remaining open to different interpretations of that Scripture). One must also be keenly alert to false values which so easily creep into the study of human nature, particularly the contemporary preoccupation with self as Hinman, Kilpatrick, Vitz and others have pointed out (see Chapter 7). Nevertheless, all truth, whether it is found in the Scriptures as special revelation, or in creation as general revelation, is God's truth and is equally trustworthy. This is both a comforting thought when one is faced with apparent disagreement between psychology and Christianity, and a thrilling thought when one realizes one is studying God's highest creation--a reflection of God Himself!

Levels of explanation. This position recognizes the continuity between God acting in Scripture and God as He continues to act. It also recognizes that events can be described and explained on different levels. An explanation on one level does not "explain away" an explanation on another. When I bow my head, close my eyes, and direct my thoughts in a certain way, a physiological psychologist can explain the events in terms of changing brain wave patterns and the sending of neural impulses from the motor strip on the cortex, along nerve pathways to the relevant muscles in the eyes and neck. A cognitive psychologist could describe the thought patterns involved and the changing level of consciousness as a "meditative" state being achieved. An analytic psychologist might explain my behavior as an attempt by my conscious self to become attuned to the god archetype in my collective unconscious. Each of these explanations stands independent of the others and offers potentially useful insights. None of them however, precludes a further

10

explanation of my behavior as communication between myself and God on a spiritual level--prayer.

All of this is not to say there are no legitimate grounds for disagreement between psychology and Christianity. Contemporary North American psychology (the humanists notwithstanding) rests heavily on positivist, materialist, empiricist assumptions. That is, it restricts itself to what can be observed through the physical senses. In this it fails to heed the admonition of one of its most respected authors, William James:

> Science, however, must be constantly reminded that her purposes are not the only purposes, and that the order of uniform causation which she has use for, and is therefore right in postulating, may be enveloped in a wider order, on which she has no claim at all. (1890, 576)

The Christian may recognize this "wider order" as a spiritual dimension which interacts continuously with the material "order of uniform causation." This "wider order" is ignored by most contemporary psychologists. Even psychologists studying religion (including William James) necessarily restrict themselves to the scientific study of religion and its role in the individual's life, without venturing into metaphysical speculation (or revelation).

In its attempt to be scientific, psychology has restricted itself to the measurement and interpretation of observable data, and in so doing has cut itself off from many of its own rich religious/philosophical roots. This does not mean that psychology is of no use, but only that it is description and explanation **at one level only**--a fact which needs to be recognized by both sides of the psychology/Christianity debate.

The beauty, the orderliness, the love that we see all point to God (just as the ugliness, the chaos, and hate point to sin). This is seen very clearly in humans, who have both divine and creaturely (not to mention sinful) characteristics. We may see psychologists with their various areas of interest and their various theories as somewhat

11

like the blind men who encountered an elephant: one grasped the trunk and said, "Why an elephant is like a huge writhing snake," another touched the elephant's side and said "No, an elephant is like a rough flat wall," a third encountered the elephant's leg and said "Obviously an elephant is like the trunk of a tree"--each one was correct but each description was incomplete. Similarly with psychology, even the spiritually "blind" secular psychologists may be accurate within the limitations of their points of view.

Summary. We may say then, that both the fear of many Christians, and the skepticism of many secular psychologists have several possible sources. The main ones would seem to be the following:[1]

1. Sometimes the criticisms of the secular psychologists are legitimate.[2]

2. Both sides often fail to recognize the tentative nature of the application of scientific principles to psychology, valuable and necessary though they be as working assumptions (Paloutzian, 1983).

3. There is often a failure to appreciate different explanations for a single behavior as being on different "levels" and hence complementary rather than contradictory (Myers, 1983, 7-8).

4. Finally, part of the "cultural baggage" inherited by contemporary evangelicals from their fundamentalist forebears is a view of the world which makes a sharp split between secular and sacred. This has frequently resulted in a fear of the findings of science, including scientific psychology, which is a failure to recognize all truth as God's truth.

---

[1]. For a more detailed discussion see Carter and Narramore, 1979; Paloutzian, 1983, 95 ff.

[2]. For example see Narramore, 1984, 137 ff regarding the excessive use of guilt motivation by Christians.

12

How then can psychology and Christianity be related? By recognizing God at work in both. The following assumptions are suggested as a basis upon which this relationship rests:

1. Jesus Christ, as the Son of God, is the most complete revelation of God to humanity.

2. God has revealed Himself in His dealings with humanity as recorded in Scripture.

3. Since God created the universe, including humanity, these too are a resource for knowledge about God and His ways.

4. God endows people with a capacity for reason which enables them to extend their understanding (within limits) of God's ongoing creation.

5. Psychology, as a study of persons made in the image of God, although fallen, is a valid source of understanding about creation, and an indirect source of knowledge about God.

6. Where Scripture speaks of the supernatural realm, psychology must be silent; where it speaks clearly and unmistakably of the natural realm it is paramount; where interpretation involving human knowledge and reason is necessary, all revelation, both scriptural and "natural," should be considered.

7. The **interpretation** of Scripture is as much a fallible human enterprise as the interpretation of any other data, including psychology. Although the study of Scripture has an unquestionably higher object than psychology (thus theology is the "Queen of Sciences"), this does not make its practioners any less fallible. Where interpretation is necessary, and fallible human reason is involved, albeit guided by the Holy Spirit, other sources of knowledge, which are also from God, must be responsibly considered.

The relationship which is proposed here is often reciprocal and thus mutually beneficial. For example, Scripture says "spare the rod and spoil the child." This may be (and has been) literally interpreted to mean that physical punishment using a rod is always necessary. However, psychological

13

research indicates that physical punishment, in some situations at least, has undesirable effects. This may lead us to re-examine our **interpretation** of the Scripture. Perhaps it is emphasizing the importance of discipline and not necessarily a particular type. When we examine Scripture further we find that this re-interpretation is consistent with other areas. For example, punishment in Scripture is not always with a physical rod, it is not always even primarily physical (being cut off from one's family and nation is a severe punishment, and separation from God is the ultimate punishment). Thus a complimentary relationship between Scripture and psychology is found.

The limited nature of the reciprocity between Scripture and psychology is illustrated if this example is extended to consider the possibility that psychology might conclude that all punishment is undesirable (as B.F. Skinner does). This would clearly be contrary to any interpretation of Scripture and would lead the Christian psychologist to search further for a better interpretation of the psychological data. In this way psychology may guide scriptural interpretation, and Scripture may guided psychological research.

CHRISTIAN PSYCHOLOGY TODAY

Although the issues which we have seen trouble the relationship between psychology and Christianity are not resolved, they are receiving an increased amount of attention. As more and more Christians turn to psychology for help and as more and more Christians are trained in psychology, there is increasing pressure to resolve the relationship issues and develop a unified "Christian psychology." What then is the current status of Christian psychology? Has it developed to the point where it may be considered a significant force?

> Is there a Christian school of
> psychology?

In exploring this issue we will leave the more theoretical questions with which we have been dealing, and turn to more practical questions. First, we will define a "school" of psychology, and then survey several schools, and finally review the evidence for a uniquely Christian school.

SCHOOLS OF PSYCHOLOGY

The term "school" as it is used in the study of the history of psychology, and as we are using it here, indicates a system or movement within psychology.

> The term **school** refers to a group of psychologists who become associated ideologically, and sometimes geographically, with the leader of a movement. For the most part, the members of a school work on common problems and share a theoretical or systematic orientation .(Schulz, 1981, 12)

The first systematic position in psychology was known as structuralism. The early structuralists (Wilhelm Wundt in Germany, and E.B. Titchener in the United States) attempted to analyse conscious experience into separate parts and so discover the nature or **structure** of consciousness. Consciousness, which had taken on the role occupied by "mind" or "soul" in the older philosophies, became the object of intense scientific investigation.

However, trying to analyse consciousness in terms of its component parts did not prove very fruitful, and the goal of many psychologists soon changed to discovering the **function** of consciousness. The new "functionalists" were greatly influenced by Darwin's theory of evolution and began to analyse mental processes in terms of their adaptive functions for the changing organism. They also began to investigate animal behavior having concluded that there was a great deal more similarity between animals and humans than had previously been assumed. Consciousness (mind, soul) had been shifted from center-stage" and it remained for "behaviorism" to shift it "off stage" entirely.

15

In 1913 John Watson wrote an article for the Psychological Review called "Psychology as the Behaviorist Views it" and began a revolution in psychology. As he put it, "The time seems to have come when psychology must discard all reference to consciousness," and furthermore, "The behaviorist, ...recognizes no dividing line between man and brute." Reacting to what he saw as the failure of current schools in psychology, Watson proposed a fresh new approach. Psychology must be entirely objective, relying only on repeatable, verifiable observations. The only suitable object of study for a scientific psychology was behavior, behavior of all types, animal and human, but only behavior. All mentalistic concepts were rejected,-- consciousness, mind, thinking. Although there has been a return to some of the concepts Watson rejected, such as consciousness, contemporary psychology remains heavily influenced by the objective methods of behaviorism.

Although it has always remained somewhat outside of the sphere of general psychology, psychoanalysis as developed by Sigmund Freud has had a significant impact upon psychology generally and may also be considered a "school." Because it was developed primarily as a method of therapy its influence within psychology has been primarily in the areas of personality theory and psychotherapy.

The most recent development within psychology which could be considered a school is humanistic psychology. This "third force" developed largely as a reaction to the limited views of behaviorism and psychoanalysis. In many ways it represents a return to earlier interests in psychology.

> The emphasis on conscious experience, the wholeness of human nature and conduct, the belief in free will and spontaneity, the creative power of the individual, and the study of all that is relevant to the human condition--can be found in the works of older psychologists (Schulz, 1981, 381)

. Although this movement has been in existence for over 30 years, and continues to grow in

16

influence, it by no means dominates the field of psychology as some earlier movements have.

These then are the major schools which have produced contemporary psychology.[1] They have been the result of both great men (e.g., Watson, Freud) and the social/intellectual climate of their times (e.g., the theory of evolution, American pragmatism).

The forces which produce a movement in psychology are varied; they include the "zeitgeist," or spirit of the times, the influence of great leaders, and often an existing school or movement against which to react. Schools rise to prominance by publishing books, establishing journals, and training graduate students in the ideas of the founder(s).

A CHRISTIAN SCHOOL OF PSYCHOLOGY?

The last decade has seen many of the forces which have produced other schools of psychology act towards producing a Christian school of psychology. The "zeitgeist" has swung from the narrow and restrictive view of humanity espoused by functionalism and particularly behaviorism towards the high view taken by humanism. Christian psychology also takes a very high view of humanity. Although differing with the humanists on the innate goodness of humanity, Christian psychologists see people as the tarnished but potentially redeemable image of God. Among secular humanists some of the euphoria over the potential of humanity may now bewearing off leaving a greater openness to a Christian view.

Christian psychologists have also begun to speak out more frequently and effectively. Probably the best known of these is James Dobson with his numerous books, international radio broadcast, and popular film series. Many other

---

1. Other forces have combined to produce contemporary psychology (e.g., Gestalt psychology), and new movements continue to develop (e.g., cognitive psychology--cf. Chapter 6). However, the most influential movements have been noted. Further discussion is beyond the scope of the present work.

17

Christian psychologists are also publishing books, so that a quick glance through any Christian bookstore will reveal a vast array of titles by Christian psychologists on a wide variety of topics. [1]

Several seminaries and Christian colleges have begun to offer not only majors but also complete graduate programs in psychology. Probably the best known of these is Rosemead Graduate School of Professional Psychology at Biola University near Los Angeles. [2] This school has been accredited by the American Psychological Association and offers the traditional Ph.D. degree in psychology as well as an applied doctorate of psychology (Psy.D.). Rosemead is particularly interesting for our discussion here because not only is it the largest evangelical Christian school of psychology but it is also a leader in the study of the relationship between psychology and Christianity. Several of its faculty list this subject as one of their major interests and have published in the area. Professors Narramore, Carter, and Fleck edit an ongoing series of books dealing with the integration of psychology and Christian faith, "The Rosemead Psychology Series" (published by Zondervan). Rosemead professors William F. Hunter and Richard J, Mohline also edit the Journal of Psychology and Theology, which deals extensively with integration issues.

Thus Christian psychology as represented by Rosemead is probably the closest thing to a new school of psychology as that term is traditionally used. It may be seen as a reaction to existing secular schools; it has its leaders who are publishing and training graduate students; it has founded a significant journal and an ongoing series of larger publications. But is it truly a

---

1. See the "References and Other Sources" at the end of this chapter for a small sampling.

2. Rosemead is used here as an example. Similar arguments, both pro and con, could be applied to other significant centers of Christian psychology such as Fuller and Wheaton.

new "school of psychology" capable of speaking as the voice of Christian psychology?

Although many of the characteristics of other schools of psychology exist with regard to Rosemead, it would be premature to speak of a unified Christian psychology at this time for two reasons. First, Rosemead is relatively unknown outside of Christian circles; its publications are only rarely found in secular bookstores and libraries, and it has provoked very little if any reaction among secular psychologists generally. Second, there are several other significant efforts being made to work out a Christian psychology, and no consensus has yet emerged from these diverse efforts (to which fact the topics of this book are a testimony). Although The Journal of Psychology and Theology has as its primary purpose the relating of psychology and theology, significant articles on this subject from slightly different perspectives also appear in the Journal of Psychology and Christianity, and The Journal of the American Scientific Affiliation (soon to be Perspectives in Science and Christian Faith).

One of the main purposes of the present book is to stimulate the dialogue among thoughtful Christians on some of the important issues for them in psychology. However, the goal of this process is not so much to develop a school of psychology, but rather to promote critical evaluation of contemporary psychology on a broad scale so that fragmentation does not occur and many different "schools" or antagonistic movements develop within Christian psychology. The psychologists at Rosemead are doing an admirable job in writing, editing, and training graduates. So too are many other Christian psychologists who work in Christian colleges, seminaries, institutes, secular colleges, and various applied settings. Each of these, as well as the informed Christian without graduate degrees, has something to contribute to the development of what is currently but an embryonic Christian psychology.

DISCUSSION QUESTIONS

Scientific method. The positivist, empiricist assumptions of science have been widely accepted in North American psychology, as it has tried to model itself after the natural sciences--especially physics. Are these assumptions appropriate given not only the complexity and reactivity of human nature, but also its spiritual dimension? Many Christians would say yes, within limitations. However, some Christian psychologists (e.g., VanLeeuwen, 1982, 1983) feel that a completely new approach is needed.[1]

Christian psychology. Perhaps related to the previous question, we might also ask should Christian psychology be unique? Most, if not all, Christian psychologists rely on secular theories to some extent. Is it satisfactory to reinterpret these from a Christian perspective or should we start at the bottom and develop a unique and original "Christian psychology" (cf. Collins, 1977)? In addition to Christian forms of therapy and personality theory, do we need Christian research methods, Christian learning theory, Christian statistics, etc.?

Christian school of psychology. Contemporary psychology shows the influence of several different "schools" from the past. Should Christian psychologists attempt to influence the development of psychology by promoting a "school of Christian psychology?" In the development of such a school how important are "great men", a geographic identity, journals?

Would the church be better served by psychology if there was a consensus among Christian psychologists on theories and methods?

In conclusion, psychology is a many faceted and continually changing attempt to understand and help people. As such it is potentially a valuable ally to the Christian. Consequently, several notable attempts are being made to develop a Christian psychology which is true to first of all the "special revelation" of Scripture, and second, the honest investigation of created "natural revelation." However, a great deal of misunderstanding still exists between psychology and Christianity, often because of prejudice on both sides. A willingness to explore the issues,

[1] See also Rosenak (1984).

20

some of which are the subject of this book, and an ability to suspend judgment until all the relevant facts are considered will go a long way towards resolving the differences. The present book is an attempt to stimulate further development in this direction.

SUGGESTED READINGS

Carter, J.D. & Narramore, B. 1979. The integration of psychology and theology. Grand Rapids: Zondervan. One of the best known and accepted analyses of the integration question. Several different approaches presented. Clear and readable.

Farnsworth, K. 1985. Wholehearted integration. Grand Rapids: Baker Book House. Good example of "state-of-the-art" integration by a Christian scholar. Theoretical and practical.

Koteskey, Ronald L. 1980. Psychology from a Christian perspective. Nashville: Abingdon. A very helpful approach to integration based on a view of humans having animal-like, God-like, and unique characteristics. Finds value in virtually every area of psychology.

Paloutzian, Raymond F. 1983. Invitation to the psychology of religion. Glenview, Il: Scott, Foresman and Company. Good introduction to the psychology of religion. Especially helpful discussion of a philosophy of science for the study of religion. (The complete Summer 1986 volume of the Journal of Psychology and Christianity is dedicated to helpful discussion of the psychology of religion.)

Van Leeuwen, M.S. 1982. The sorcerer's apprentice: A Christian looks at the changing face of psychology. Downers Grove, IL: InterVarsity Press. Criticism of psychology by an academic Christian. Suggests the "scientific paradigm" be abandoned for a "human science" paradigm. Good criticism of the use of deception in experimentation. (See also her The person in psychology for a somewhat broader but less readable source.)

REFERENCES AND OTHER SOURCES

Adams, J.E. 1971. Competent to counsel. Grand Rapids: Baker Book House.

Adams, J.E. 1973. The Christian counselor's manual. Grand Rapids: Baker Book House.

American Standard Bible. 1973. Chicago: Moody Press.

Atkinson, R.L., Atkinson, R.C. Smith, E.E., & Hilgard, E.R. 1987. Introduction to psychology, (9th ed.). New York: Harcourt Brace Jovanovich.

Burnham, J.C. 1985. The encounter of Christian theology with deterministic psychology and psychoanalysis. Bulletin of the Menninger Clinic, 49, 321-352.

Carter, J.D. & Narramore, B. 1979. The integration of psychology and theology. Grand Rapids: Zondervan.

Collins, G.R. 1977. The rebuilding of psychology: An integration of psychology and Christianity. Wheaton Il: Tyndale House.

Collins, G.R. 1981. Psychology and theology: Prospects for integration. Nashville: Abingdon.

Crabb, Lawrence J., Jr. 1977. Effective biblical counselling. Grand Rapids, MI: Zondervan.

Ellens, J. Harold. 1983. God's grace and human health. Nashville: Abingdon.

Farnsworth, K. 1981. Integrating psychology and theology: Elbows together but hearts apart. Washington, D.C.: University Press of America.

Farnsworth, K. 1982. "The conduct of integration." Journal of Psychology and Theology. 10, 308-319.

Farnsworth, K. 1985. Wholehearted integration. Grand Rapids: Baker Book House.

Hinman, N.E. 1980. An answer to humanistic psychology. Irvine, California: Harvest House Publishers.

Hsieh, T. 1982, December. Integration efforts of some Christian psychology faculty. Journal of the American Scientific Affiliation, 239-241.

Hunt, D., & McMahon, T.A. 1985. The seduction of Christianity. Eugene, OR: Harvest House.

James, William. 1890. The principles of psychology. New York: Holt.

Kilpatrick, William K. 1983. Psychological seduction. New York: Nelson.

Koteskey, Ronald L. 1980. Psychology from a Christian perspective. Nashville: Abingdon.

L'Engle, Madeleine. 1983. And it was good. Wheaton, Il: Harold Shaw.

McConnell, James, V. 1983. Understanding human behavior, (4th ed.). New York: Holt, Rinehart and Winston.

McLemore, C.W. 1982. The scandal of psychotherapy. Wheaton: Tyndale House.

McLemore, C.W. 1974. Clergyman's psychological handbook. Grand Rapids: Eerdmans.

Malony, H. N., ed. 1978. Psychology and faith: The Christian experience of eighteen psychologists. Washington: University Press of America.

Myers, David G. 1983. Social psychology. New York: McGraw-Hill.

Narramore, S. B. 1984. No condemnation. Grand Rapids: Zondervan.

Narramore, S. B. & Counts, B. 1974. Freedom from guilt. Santa Ana: Vision House.

Paloutzian, Raymond F. 1983. Invitation to the psychology of religion. Glenview, Il: Scott, Foresman and Company.

Rosenak, C.M. 1984. Christian thinking on philosophical foundations for the science of psychology. Journal of the American Scientific Affiliation, 36, 39-42.

Saltzberg, L., & Elkins, G. 1980. An examination of common concerns about rational-emotive therapy. Professional Psychology, 11, 324-330.

Schulz, Duane. 1981. A history of modern psychology, (3rd ed.). New York: Academic Press.

Van Leeuwen, M.S. 1982. The sorcerer's apprentice: A Christian looks at the changing face of psychology. Downers Grove, IL: InterVarsity Press.

Van Leeuwen, M.S. 1983. Reflexivity in North American psychology: Historical reflections on one aspect of a changing paradigm. Journal of the American Scientific Affiliation, 35, 162-167.

Van Leeuwen, M.S. 1985. The person in psychology. Grand Rapids: Eerdmans.

Vitz, Paul C. 1977. Psychology as religion: The cult of self-worship. Grand Rapids: Eerdmans.

Watson, John B. 1913. Psychology as the behaviorist views it. Psychological Review, 20, 158-177.

Journals

Journal of the American Scientific Affiliation. P.O. Box. J, Ipswich, MA 01938

Journal of Psychology and Christianity. CAPS International, 26705 Farmington Road, Farmington Hills, MI 48018.

Journal of Psychology and Theology. Rosemead School of Psychology, school of Biola University, 13800 Biola Ave., La Mirada, CA 90639

CHAPTER 2: PHYSIOLOGICAL PSYCHOLOGY

BRAIN RESEARCH
MIND OVER BODY
MIND/BODY PROBLEM
CONTROVERSIAL ISSUE

> Are some religious phenomena purely the results of activities of the body, and others purely the results of activities of the mind?

RELIGION AND THE BODY
RELIGION AND THE MIND
DISCUSSION QUESTIONS
    Mind/body problem
    Seat of the soul
    Fasting
    After-death experiences
    Comparative psychology
SUGGESTED READINGS
REFERENCES AND OTHER SOURCES

Physiological psychology studies the effects which bodily structures and processes have on thought and behavior. Because the analysis of these structures and processes is often highly technical, physiological psychology does not usually "grab" the attention of beginning students. However, Christians have an important stake in this area as the following examples show.

1. Ivan Pavlov, famous for his discovery of "classical conditioning," also discovered that dogs would learn new patterns of behavior much more rapidly while in a state of emotional/mental exhaustion brought on by over-taxing the brain. William Sargant (1957) argues that brainwashing and conversion also involve a re-orientation which is made possible by extreme emotional/mental stress. Could Christian conversion be a form of brainwashing brought on by stress to the brain?

2. After reviewing a carefully controlled study, and surveying scores of users of LSD-type drugs, W.H. Clark (1973) concludes, "In some situations and with some people, and especially when both subject and guide intend it, the psychedelic drugs release very profound religious experience of a mystical nature," and further, "There are many well-attested cases on record of dramatic, lasting conversions and religious growth of a profound nature following use of LSD-type drugs" (17-19). Could religious experience have a chemical basis?

Are electro-chemical processes in the brain alone responsible for religious conversion and mystical experiences? On the otherhand, what is the role of the self-aware, thinking, feeling part of us which we call the mind? Could it "manufacture" experiences Christians would attribute to supernatural intervention? Consider these examples:

1. In a comfortable chair, her eyes closed, with only a simple piece of electronic apparatus attached to one finger, a woman is learning to control the bodily processes that will eliminate her migraine headaches. In another part of the room a man is teaching his body to lower its blood pressure. Still another is learning to slow his heart rate.

26

These are the wonders of "bio-feedback," a technique which teaches the mind new ways to control the body.

2. Jokes, video cassettes of comedies and stand-up comics, music, poetry, drawing, and painting, are some of the aids used by Norman Cousins (1976, 1984) and others to overcome some very serious illnesses. There is a growing body of evidence that a positive "up-beat" mental attitude, as well as specific mental imaging, produces identifiable changes in the body's ability to fight disease.

Clearly the mind affects the body. But does it control the body completely? And what of "divine" healing? Is it simply a matter of the mind controlling the body?

Before considering these questions further we will review briefly some of the relevant findings under the headings of "Brain Research" and "Mind Over Body."

BRAIN RESEARCH

Your brain is the most complex system known to science. It is made up of more than 15 billion nerve cells, each of which may communicate with thousands of other cells, pushing the possible combinations of cells beyond comprehension.

Up until the last 40 or 50 years, little was known about brain functioning and neural processing beyond the relatively crude findings of animal studies. Study of the human brain was dependent upon accidents and diseases to afflict the brain, and post mortem investigation to discover causes for disturbed thought and behavior. However, recent technical advances have contributed greatly to our understanding of this complex mystery by allowing investigation of the living brain.

One of these technical advances is the electroencephalograph or EEG machine. This machine picks up small electrical impulses from tiny electrodes attached to the scalp and translates them into visual patterns on a screen or a moving piece of paper. The electrical impulses and the

27

resulting patterns are general indicators of brain activity. They show "waves" of electrical energy resulting from the discharge of many brains cells at once. These waves can be related to various general states of the individual such as problem solving, resting, sleeping, etc. but they do not indicate anything about either individual cells or specific thoughts and feelings.

A great deal of work has been done relating EEG patterns to various stages of sleep. An EEG may also be useful in diagnosing abnormal brain activity such as might result from a tumor or occur during an epileptic seizure.

Another approach to brain research has been to observe the effects of delivering a small electrical current through tiny electrodes planted deep in the brain. Robert Heath (1963), for example, found that a patient suffering from narcolepsy (a disorder which caused him to fall asleep unexpectedly, in a matter of seconds) could keep himself awake by pressing a button on a portable apparatus which caused a shock to be delivered deep in his brain. The feelings of arousal which this produced were said to be quite pleasant.

Perhaps the most intriguing line of research was that carried out by the Canadian neurosurgeon Wilder Penfield (1950, 1959). Penfield's method of helping his patients with severe forms of epilepsy was to discover and remove damaged portions of the brain (usually parts of the temporal lobe of the cerebral cortex). In order to determine the offending parts and the effects of their removal, Penfield's technique required him to probe the brain, delivering a small electrical impulse through a tiny electrode, while the patient remained conscious (the brain, which has no feeling of its own, was exposed using only a local anesthetic). Thus the patient could report to him the effects of stimulation at various points. Not only was this effective in determining the source of the epileptic discharge, but it also provided a rich source of information for mapping of the cortex (the outer layer of the cerebrum, associated with "higher" mental functions).

A startling but frequent finding was that stimulation in certain areas produced extremely vivid memories.

> There is an area of the surface of the human brain where local electrical stimulation can call back a sequence of past experience....It is as though a wire recorder, or strip of cinematographic film with a sound track, had been set in motion within the brain. The sights and sounds, and the thoughts, of a former day pass through the man's mind again. (1959, 1719)

These memories were so vivid that some patients had difficulty in believing that Penfield had not arranged for them to actually occur. Yet in spite of their vividness patients were clearly aware that they were on the operating table in Montreal, and the memory appeared as a kind of parallel experience. On one occasion,

> A young South African patient lying on the operating table exclaimed, when he realized what was happening, that it was astonishing to him to realize that he was laughing with his cousins on a farm in South Africa, while he was also fully conscious of being in the operating room in Montreal. (1975, 55)

This phenomenon of parallel experiences Penfield called "double consciousness."

Although the nerve impulse is generally described in electrical terms, its transmission between individual nerve cells (across the space between cells called a synapse) is primarily chemical. This fact has prompted a great deal of research attention to be focussed on brain chemistry. Currently chemical brain research is finding answers to important questions such as: What is the role of chemicals, particularly RNA, in storing memories? What chemical differences exist between the brains of normals and those of seriously disturbed individuals such as schizophrenics? Could learning be made easier with the use of certain chemicals? What changes in brain chemistry accompany changes in mood or attitude (e.g., the "runner's high")?

MIND OVER BODY

While brain research has focussed on the physical organism, the body, and investigated ways in which objective physical changes lead to subjective psychological changes, another branch of study has examined ways in which the subjective mind may exert control over the physical body. Probably the most popular of these is the technique of biofeedback.

Beginning with the demonstration by Eastern mystics that bodily functions such as heart rate, previously thought beyond control, could in fact be consciously controlled, modern psychology has sought a quick and easy way of accomplishing this control. They found it in biofeedback.

Biofeedback involves using electronic amplification and analysis of bodily functions so that changes in these functions can be monitored by the individual himself or herself. Thus, for example, a person may be attached to apparatus which emits a particular sound when his or her blood pressure increases and another sound when it decreases. Through practice he or she learns the particular internal responses necessary to control these changes. Similar procedures may be used to bring under voluntary control heart rate, or temperature in the hands (which was discovered to be inversely related to migraine headaches). In this way biofeedback has provided a powerful tool for the mind in acquiring greater conscious control of the body.

A somewhat less reliable situation of "mind over matter" is seen in the use of placebos (a non-medicated pill made of sugar or flour). While the effectiveness of placebos to reduce pain has been known for centuries, recent research (Gordon and Levine, 1981) has indicated that this effect is more than imaginary. Evidence suggests that an individual's expectation of reduced pain may actually cause his or her body to generate its own natural pain killers (called endorphins). While placebos are usually effective in less than one-half of the cases, the effects they produce are very real.

In a similar vein, there is increasing evidence to indicate that definite biochemical changes in the body's immune system may be produced by other mental factors. Although the adverse effects of negative mental states, particularly stress, have been known for some time, the beneficial effects of positive states are just now being documented. Increases in disease fighting antibodies have been reported for not only general "positive" thinking, but also for specific imaging or picturing of the body's disease fighting mechanisms successfully battling the invading organisms (Hall, 1982-83; Hammer, 1984).

Thus there is ample evidence to support the conclusion that the mind may exert a powerful control over the body.

MIND/BODY PROBLEM

In this brief review of the research we have noted first the physical basis of certain mental events and second some ways in which mental events may have internal physical consequences. That is, we have shown both that the body affects the conscious mind and that the conscious mind affects the body. In the historic philosophical discussion of the mind/body problem, (which is basically "Are the mind and body of two different substances, and if so do they interact?") the evidence reviewed seems to be most consistent with the position known as dualistic interactionism. This position asserts that the body and the mind are of fundamentally different natures or essences, which nevertheless interact in humans.

Psychologists do not normally talk about the mind surviving death, or being capable of communication with God, but rather they focus on characteristics such as creativity, intelligence, and self-awareness. However, with the exception of the concepts of survival and communication with God, psychologists mean basically the same thing by the term "mind" as Christians do by the term "soul," or even "spirit," that is, the immaterial expression of a unique self-awareness which while currently dependent upon a material body, survives the destruction of the body, and which at this immaterial level may interact with God by whom it was created. Thus the mind/body problem is basically the soul/body problem as it was

31

originally, and the question becomes once again "How does the soul interact with the body?"

Having seen that the body and mind exert a strong influence on each other, and having suggested that the Christian concept of the soul is involved, let us now return to some of the questions raised at the beginning of this chapter.

CONTROVERSIAL ISSUE

Sargant (1957) has suggested that conversion is a result of increased suggestibility following brain over-load. Clark (1973) claims that drugs may produce religious experiences. Can neurobiology and biochemistry account for religious experience?

Through an act of the will the mind can obtain vast control over the body, directing vital functions, and even fighting disease. Could "divine" healing be simply a matter of mind over body?

These questions may be summarized in the following way:

> Are some religious phenomena purely the results of activities of the body, and others purely the results of activities of the mind?

We turn first to the body as the source of religious experience, and then the mind.

RELIGION AND THE BODY

In dealing with the specific issues raised by Sargant and Clark, there are three more general points that we need to consider:

1. Although body and mind (or soul) may be of entirely different essences, the dominant view of humans in Scripture seems to be of a holistic body-soul unit (thus the crucial importance of a

32

resurrection).[1] Therefore it should not surprise us that physiological events may have mental and spiritual ramifications. It is a working assumption of physiological psychologists, and one that is not necessarily unacceptable to Christians, that every experience of the individual has a physiological correlate. Whether you are talking, thinking, or merely passively conscious without any focus of attention, your brain is actively monitoring, responding to, and recording your experience. As the Christian brain researcher Donald MacKay describes this assumption,

> For every feature of our conscious experience...there is some correlate in the physical activity of our brains, causally linked with prior brain activity and incoming sensory information....What we are saying is that these aspects are complementary. They are not exactly symmetrical, since there can be some changes of brain-state without any change of conscious experience, whereas the converse (we believe) is not the case. (1980, 82-83)

Thus we may expect that not only conversion, but religious experiences of every kind may have physiological, probably cerebral, correlates. And, we might add, Christians need not fear advances in our understanding of these physiological correlates to religious experience. In MacKay's words,

> I would argue that Christians as such have no justification in Scripture for postulating any sort of barrier to the progress of brain science. 'Physical', 'mental' and 'spiritual' are complementary categories, all of which are embraced by the totality of what it is to be a man. (1974, 72-73)

2. Although brain research is justified, and even to be welcomed, we need to keep in mind the dangers of "nothing-buttery" (as noted in Chapter 1). That is, because an experience has a physiological explanation does not mean that it is nothing but physiology; other levels of explanation may be equally valid. Even the notable

---

[1]   For a discussion of dualism and holism in Scripture see Weathers (1983).

neurophysiologists Wilder Penfield and Sir John Eccles, who throughout their careers operated under the assumption that the brain was the origin of all experience, were compelled toward the end of their careers to propose another level of being which may interact with the physiological level (Custance, 1980).

Returning to Sargant's example, the fact that a religious conversion followed mental distress does not mean that there were not other, perhaps more important, contributing factors of an entirely different nature. Explanation at the physiological level does not rule out explanations at other, non-physical levels--for example the convicting power of the Holy Spirit.

The same is true with regard to Clark's claim that drugs may aid in religious experience. While there may be irrefutable arguments against the advisability of using drugs, and while we may be able to point to chemical bases for their effects, nevertheless, these considerations alone do not mean the religious experiences they occasionally produced were therefore invalid.

3. We must always be open to the possibility that the critics may be right--at least in some instances. When physiological and psychological explanations are given for the religious experiences of cultists, such as the snake handlers in the southern U.S., Christians do not usually object. We need to be open to the possibility that some well meaning Christians may also misuse physiological and psychological means towards their own good ends. As Martyn Lloyd-Jones (1959) points out, Sargant has done us a service by alerting us to this possibility. There is ample evidence in the writings of Wesley, Finney, Edwards, and Whitfield, that they at times were guilty of using psychological "techniques." Lloyd-Jones says of Whitfield,

> He allowed his own eloquence and his own imagination to run away with him. He reached a point at which he was not so much presenting the message of the gospel as producing an oratorical, not to say psychological, effect upon his congregation. (34)

When we use such "effects" we do the cause of Christ a disservice, leaving ourselves open to the charge of manipulation, and producing converts of doubtful endurance.

To summarize, in answer to the first part of our original question, it appears that while all religious experience may be expected to have corresponding physiological processes, such experiences may also be much more than just these processes.

RELIGION AND THE MIND

In considering religion and the mind we are concerned with the question, "Are some religious phenomena purely the result of activities of the mind?" In particular, we raised the issue earlier of whether healings described as "divine" might not be the result of purely mental processes. For purposes of this discussion we will limit ouselves to consideration of those cases where there is a verifiable change in physical symptoms.

Having determined previously that beliefs, attitudes, and expectations can produce physical cures, we must admit that these factors can never be ruled out whether or not the person is also taking medication, praying to God, Buddha, or his or her ancestors. In the Christian context where prayer is offered, psychological factors are always a confounding variable, making it virtually impossible to determine the precise role of supernatural intervention.

While this fact makes careful scientific analysis difficult, there is no reason to avoid it. On the contrary, in as much as God not only created the universe but continues to uphold it "by the word of His power," working not only through extraordinary, "supernatural" means, but also through natural laws whether of medicine or psychology, Christians should be encouraged to make use of these laws. Positive thoughts promote healing just as in some cases an antibiotic medicine

35

does.[1] Whether in sickness or in health Christians can profit from the application of God's laws.

If it were possible to observe that a prayer for healing was followed by increased hope and desire to live, as well as other positive and uplifting thoughts, which in turn was followed by a strengthening of the body's immune system and defeat of the disease, would we not be obliged to thank God? Healing is from God, whether we have a glimpse of the intervening processes or not.

There is however another issue which may be raised here. Having discovered the power of the mind, and admitted its value to Christians, there is perhaps a danger that we may come to rely on it, even inadvertently, and so exclude the supernatural work of God. This is the position advanced by Watchman Nee (1972) in his little book "The Latent Power of the Soul."

Nee argues that many amazing occurrences attributed to God by contemporary Christians are simply the result of the power of the soul (mind), particularly the power of souls in agreement. For example, if your prayer is directed towards another individual, perhaps thousands of miles away, that she come to God, the prayers may be effective in oppressively forcing her to God. But God is not in it; it was your soul power which directed your desires to the other individual and compelled her. While we may not wish to go so far as Nee in condemning the use of mental powers, it is an area for careful study and consideration by Christians. We need to be aware of the power of the mind, its potential for use and abuse.

To summarize, we have examined some interesting claims arising from the area of physiological psychology and seen that a more thorough understanding of the area generates helpful insight rather than conflict in the relationship between psychology and Christianity. Acquaintance with physiological psychology, as with other areas, provides the thoughtful Christian

---

1. "A merry heart doeth good like a medicine" (Prov. 17:22; see also Phil. 4:8).

with important background knowledge he or she needs to evaluate claims relating to this area.

Such knowledge would produce a healthy skepticism which is sometimes lacking, as the following example shows. A concerned student recently gave me a clipping from a Christian prophecy newsletter (which reprinted the report from the "Christian Inquirer" magazine, March, 1985), claiming that scientists had succeeded in implanting a tiny computer in the brain of human subjects. In one case the computer was said to monitor brain waves and deliver an electric jolt when thoughts with criminal intent were recorded. In another case the computer was said to store a list of formulas to be drawn on as needed. Knowledge of the nature of neural processing and the complexity of brain activity would lead the informed layperson to be highly skeptical of such reports.

Investigation of physiological psychology also leads to an appreciation of the strength of the interaction between mind and body. Whether one considers the mind and body as two different "substances" or as different manifestations of the same substance (as in Donald MacKay's analogy of inner and outer sides of a curved line) it is clear from both science and scripture that both mind and body are integral components of personhood and neither can be ignored, especially in the discussion of religious experience.

Understanding of the interdependence of mind and body should lead Christians to a respect for the study of the body, an appreciation for the power of the mind, and an aversion to abuses of their interdependence. The body can have a tremendous and beneficial influence on the mind, but manipulation of the mind through the body, for example, using stress or drugs, demands careful consideration (see comments below regarding fasting). Similarly, the mind is a valuable aid to the health of the body, but reliance on the mind to the exclusion of physical aid (as in Christian Science) or to the exclusion of supernatural aid is also wrong.

DISCUSSION QUESTIONS

The following issues arising from the study of physiological psychology are also of interest in relating psychology and Christianity.

Mind/body problem. In this chapter we have touched on one of the oldest issues in philosophy, the question of the relationship between mind and body. This is one of the questions which psychology inherited in its development from philosophy. In our discussion we took a position known as "dualistic interactionism" (although MacKay's "comprehensive realism" is an acceptable alternative). This position sees mind and body as distinct but interacting elements (MacKay sees mind and body as different perspectives on the same element). Whether of two "essences" or one, mind and body are closely related in a scriptural view of humans (thus the stress on a physical resurrection), with the mind being capable of influencing the body as well as the body the mind.

This is not the position of much of contemporary psychology. Many psychologists view the subjective experience of conscious awareness (mind), as simply a by-product of neural functioning in the brain. They may say that mental events are identical with and nothing but brain activity, or they may say that the mind is a kind of side-show ("epiphenomenon") to the main event which is brain activity. In either case they deny that the mind has any ability to affect brain and other physiological activity.

As Christians we recognize the dependence of the mind on the body, yet we believe not only that the mind may exert its own influence on the body, but also that the mind, (i.e., the soul), survives the body's death, either through uninterrupted conscious existence or through union with a resurrected "glorified" body. Can we make this belief comprehensible to contemporary scientists?

Speculating on this question the great neurosurgeon Wilder Penfield suggested that in the absence of energy from the brain the mind might

38

establish connection with a source of energy outside the measurable world, that is, from God.[1]

An analogy suggested by MacKay (and Penfield) may also be helpful. If we see the brain as a sophisticated computer, and the mind as a programmer for the computer, then the essential uniqueness of the individual resides in the programmer (and its programs) and not the computer. Thus the computer may be destroyed, and providing the programmer is given some vehicle of expression, the individual lives on.[2]

Seat of the soul. Rene Descartes, the 17th century French philosopher who most clearly proposed a dualistic view of the person in modern times, speculated that the mind (soul) interacted with the body through the tiny pineal gland deep in the brain. Sir John Eccles has suggested liason through the pre-frontal lobe of the dominant hemisphere of the brain, whereas Wilder Penfield suggests the upper brain stem much lower in the brain. In an unpublished talk given at Trinity Western College in Langley B.C. (March 27, 1984), physiological psychologist Dr. Judith Manley Toronchuk of Regent College in Vancouver cited evidence that the brain area known as the hippocampus may be an "interface between us and the Holy Spirit."

Is there a specific part of the brain which is the "seat of the soul"? In popular language we speak of someone with extensive brain damage being "just a vegetable." But brain damage can vary through a whole continuum of severity, including not only motor dysfunctions but also gross distortions of personality. How is the soul affected, or more precisely is moral responsibility affected, and at

---

1. Penfield, W. (1975). The mystery of the mind. Princeton: Princeton University Press.

2. As a stimulant to discussion of this topic one might consider the highly unlikely scenario of a brain transplant, or more specifically, a brain swap. If you volunteered for such an experiment, how would you expect to be affected? Which person would you be?

what point does brain damage cause the soul to depart?[3]

Fasting. Going without food for long periods of time (fasting) is an important part of many religions including Christianity. Obviously there are extensive physiological changes taking place in the body as it adjusts to lack of food. What is the role of the physical changes in the heightened religious awareness? Are the physical changes a primary source of the religious experience? Are they simply a part of the experience? Or are they merely an insignificant accompaniment, with the primary function of fasting lying in other areas such as reduced social interaction and increased self discipline? Are there clues here as to some bodily functions which may inhibit and others which may promote religious experience?

After-death experiences. In recent years numerous reports have surfaced on people who claim to have had certain experiences after being declared "clinically dead" (Moody, 1975; Rawlings, 1978). The similarity among these experiences has prompted many people to consider them valid evidence of life after death.

As Christians we need to avoid two extremes in evaluating these and other unusual claims. On the one hand we must avoid rejection of legitimate evidence simply because it does not seem to fit our scheme of things, and on the other hand we must avoid premature acceptance of untested claims simply because they seem to bolster our position. At least some of the experiences related by those who have "clinically died" are explainable on the basis of known physiological processes of a body under these conditions of extreme physiological stress. Of course a physiological explanation does not rule out other explanations nor does it account for the more rare reports of the "dead" person viewing happenings in another room while "dead."

What, if anything, do after-death experiences show about the relationship between mind and

---

3. For a helpful discussion of these and related issues see "Our fragile brains" by D. Gareth Jones (1981).

body, and the ability of the mind to survive bodily death?

Comparative psychology. Comparative psychology is an area of study which is usually associated with physiological psychology. This area examines and compares the human organism with animals, noting both similarities and differences. Christians concerned with relating psychology and Christianity in comparative psychology may pose the question "What are the essential differences between animals and humans (as the "fallen" image of God), and do these differences have a physiological basis?"

Koteskey (1980) follows Francis Schaeffer (1968) in suggesting that Christians in comparative psychology have an informative comparison not only with lower levels (animals) but also with the highest level (the glorified Christ).

In conclusion, the area of physiological psychology, so often slighted by beginning students in psychology, offers a tremendous challenge to the Christian. It is here that the important groundwork for a Christian view of the person is laid, for the assumptions that are made on the relationship between mind and body directly affect the interpretation of a wide variety of religious phenomena. The relating of psychology and Christianity will not proceed very far unless the issues raised by physiological psychology are faced (either implicitly or explicitly).

SUGGESTED READINGS

Custance A. 1980. The_mysterious_matter_of_mind. Grand Rapids: Zondervan. An excellent little volume on the mind/body problem from a Christian perspective.

Jones, D.G. (1981). Our_fragile_brains. Downers Grove: InterVarsity Press. A thorough discussion of brain research by a Christian neuroscientist. Grapples with the relationship of brain processes to our understanding of the person and our relationship to God. (For a somewhat more philosophical approach see MacKay, 1980.)

41

Penfield, W. 1975. The_mystery_of_the_mind. Princeton: Princeton University Press. Interesting book by a prominent neurosurgeon. Reflecting on a life-time of probing the brain he concludes the mind is more than the brain.

REFERENCES AND OTHER SOURCES

Ashbrook, J.B. 1984. "Juxtaposing the brain and belief." Journal_of_Psychology_and_Theology, 12, 198-207.

Clark, W., Malony, H., Daane, J., & Tippett, A. 1973. Religious_experience:_Its_nature_and function_in_the_human_psyche. Springfield, IL: Thomas.

Cousins, N. 1976. Anatomy of an illness (as perceived by the patient). New England Journal_of_Medicine, 295, 1458-63.

Cousins, N. 1983. The_healing_heart. Boston: Hall and Co.

Custance A. 1980. The_mysterious_matter_of_mind. Grand Rapids: Zondervan.

Gordon, N. & Levine, J. 1981. Physiological substrates of placebo analgesia. Psychopharmacology_Bulletin, 17, 76-77.

Hall, H. 1982-83. Hypnosis and the immune system: A review with implications for cancer and the psychology of healing. American Journal_of_Clinical_Hypnosis, 25, 92-103.

Hammer, S. 1984. The mind as healer. Science Digest, 92, 47-49, 100.

Heath, R. 1963. Electrical self-stimulation of the brain in man. American_Journal_of_Psychiatry, 120, 571-77.

Jones, D.G. (1981). Our_fragile_brains. Downers Grove: InterVarsity Press.

Koteskey, R. 1980. Psychology_from_a_Christian perspective. Nashville: Abingdon.

Levine, J., Gordon, N., & Fields, H. 1978. The mechanism of placebo analgesia. Lancet, 2, 654-57.

Lloyd-Jones, M. 1959. Conversions:_Psychological and_spiritual. London: Inter-Varsity.

Lundahl, C.R., ed., 1982. A_collection_of_near-death_research_readings. Chicago: Nelson-Hall.

MacKay, D. 1974. The_clockwork_image. London: Inter-Varsity Press.

MacKay, D. 1980. Brains, machines and persons. Grand Rapids, MI: Eerdmans.

Moody, R., Jr. 1975. Life after life. New York: Bantam Books.

Nee, W. 1972. The latent power of the soul. New York: Christian Fellowship Publishers.

Penfield, W., & Rasmussen, T. 1950. The cerebral cortex of man. New York: Macmillan.

Penfield, W. 1959. The interpretive cortex. Science, 129, 1719-25.

Penfield, W. 1975. The mystery of the mind. Princeton: Princeton University Press.

Rawlings, M. 1978. Beyond death's door. New York: Bantam Books.

Sargant, W. 1957. Battle for the mind. Toronto: Heinemann.

Schaeffer, F. (1968). The God who is there. Downers Grove: Intervarsity Press.

CHAPTER 3: SENSATION AND PERCEPTION

How are Christians to evaluate claims of unusual perception?

"The Bible warns us against being misled by self-professed psychics" (Christian psychologist David Myers, 1984, p.57).

"Perhaps Christians have been too quick to reject this area of study....Most Christians believe in a 'supernatural parapsychology' with God as the intermediary force....the possibility also exists of a 'natural parapsychology' as well" (Christian psychologist Ronald Koteskey, 1980, p.74)

"Can I be persuaded by messages of which I'm not aware--messages projected rapidly or faintly on a movie screen, messages played very softly in a super-market, messages recorded backwards on records?" (numerous psychology students).

The area of psychology which studies sensation and perception contains some of the most interesting, misunderstood, and controversial topics in psychology today. As the quotations above indicate, this is no less true for Christians than for non-Christians interested in psychology.

After a brief definition of the general area, we will turn to some of the research on "subliminal perception" and "extra-sensory perception," dealing with the controversial issue:

How are Christians to evaluate claims of unusual perception?

SENSATION VERSUS PERCEPTION

Taste, touch, smell, hearing and sight, these are our five "windows on the world"--and the view they give us is spectacular! Yet they are more than just windows. Their loss means not only inconvenience but frequently emotional trauma and paranoia. Consider hearing for example. Our ears enable us to receive information not only from our immediate environment, but also from a distance, behind barriers, and behind our backs. It is a rich

46

source of social information, signalling not only the approach of others but subtle cues in their communication as well. The loss of hearing frequently produces feelings of isolation, fear and suspicion. Diminished sensation has far reaching effects--even to the disruption of mental health.

So closely are our sensations and our thoughts about our sensations related that we have difficulty separating them. My thirteen year old daughter recently asked me, "Dad, how do we know that we experience the same thing when we look at something we call 'red'?" Of course we don't, but our attempts to pin down an answer to this question may help to highlight an important distinction between sensation and perception.

Examination of the eye, optic nerve and brain indicates that transmission of visual messages is virtually identical from person to person. Thus we may safely conclude that the "sensation," the message reaching the brain, is the same for each of us when we look at something called "red." However, each of us has had different experiences with red objects, and so may have quite different responses to the same sensation. Some of us may look at a roundish red object and "see" an apple; others with different experience may "see" a mango, or a ball of red clay. The experience of "roundness" and "redness" is a sensation, the almost immediate interpretation (apple, etc.) is a perception.[1]

The distinction between sensory information, and the interpretation of that information is one which psychologist have found very useful. The study of sensation is the study of the organs, neural pathways, and brain structures associated with

---

[1]. While the distinction between pure sensation and interpretation of the sensation presents little problem theoretically, there is not universal agreement on whether or not the terms "sensation" and "perception" can be distinguished this way (i.e., some would say, "sensation is perception"). We are following Thomas Reid (1785) and most "Introductory Psychology" texts in making the distinction. For further discussion of the distinction as a problem see Coran, Porac & Ward, (1984), or other "Sensation and Perception" texts.

taste, touch, smell, hearing, sight, as well as the sense of bodily movement and balance (kinesthetic and equilibratory sense). It is that branch of physiological psychology (Chapter 2) which deals with the sensory systems.

The study of perception on the other hand, is the study of the individual's interpretive response to the messages from his or her sense organs. These responses are affected by environmental conditions, as well as the expectations and past experience of the perceiver.

Much as we would like to believe that our perceptions are an accurate mirror of reality, this is just not so. Most of us have encountered optical illusions, drawings or pictures which are clear enough to our eyes, but which we interpret incorrectly.[1] We experience the most common visual illusion when we watch a "movie," which of course is a series of still pictures projected so rapidly one after the other that the illusion of movement is generated (just as a series of blinking lights may appear as one light moving). While illusions such as these illustrate that perception is not always an accurate reflection of reality, the discrepancy is harmless.

In fact, perceptual "inaccuracies" can be very helpful. We "perceive" a coin as a constant round shape, even though our "sensation" (visual image) of it is frequently elliptical as we view it from different angles. We "perceive" a mountain as very large even though our "sensation" of it is very small from a distance. These "constancies" as they are called, are the result of past experience with similar objects in our environment. Experience has taught us that certain environmental conditions produce changes in sensation which should be overlooked or combined with other information to yield a more accurate or useful perception.

---

[1]. Familiar optical illusions are the "Abe Lincoln" hat which appears taller than the width of the brim, but is not; or the identical lines which appear longer when arrowheads point towards their ends than when they point away from them.

Because of the dependence of perception on experience, lack of relevant experience may produce dramatic perceptual deficits. Turnbull (1961; reported in Atkinson, Atkinson and Hilgard, 1983) relates the case of a Pygmy who lived in the forest where he was unable to view and approach objects from a great distance. When he was taken into open country where he saw a herd of buffalo several miles away, he thought they were insects. When they seemed to grow as he approached, he believed he was the victim of magic.

The Gospel writer Mark's account of Jesus healing the blind man (Mark 8) may also illustrate the importance of experience for accurate perception. When Jesus initially touched the man he reported seeing "men...like trees walking about." Perhaps the man's vision was blurred because the healing of the sensory apparatus was incomplete. On the other hand it may be that the man's eyes were completely healed but that he lacked the necessary experience to interpret his sensations--the problem was no longer a sensory one but a perceptual one. Such is reportedly the case of people who are given vision for the first time. Individuals born blind, who receive their sight as adults, have great difficulty in interpreting (perceiving) what they are seeing (sensing). Thus it may be that Jesus' first touch healed the man's sensory apparatus and the second touch healed his perceptual system.

SENSATION WITHOUT PERCEPTION?

In considering the controversial issue of unusual perception we will make use of the distinction we have just been discussing between sensation and perception, and consider first what might be called "sensation without perception," or more precisely, sensation and influence without conscious perception. However, before we can do this we must define the concept of "threshold" and note what it means with regard to both sensation and perception.

A threshold is the minimum level of stimulation necessary for a sensory system to be activated. A physiological threshold is the amount of physical energy necessary in a stimulus to cause the

49

receptors of a given sensory system to fire and send a message to the lower centers of the brain. A perceptual threshold is the amount of stimulation necessary for a stimulus to be consciously perceived.[1] For example, a faint sound may contain enough energy to cause a slight movement of the hearing apparatus and thus be above the physiological threshold, but not be noticed and so be below the perceptual threshold. Without this "filtering" of stimuli we would be overwhelmed by the barrage of inputs reaching the lower centers of our brain. Because most of these stimuli are irrelevant or meaningless to our conscious mind, we become "habituated" to them and ignore them (e.g., the place in your visual field occupied by your nose). Obviously, then, perceptual thresholds vary, depending upon such factors as attention, expectancy, and meaningfulness.

Subliminal perception. In the case of so-called "subliminal perception" (literally "below threshold perception"), it is claimed that stimuli which are so weak that they could not be detected even if the person tried, nevertheless influence their behavior. These stimuli which are supposedly above the physiological threshold but below the perceptual threshold, are said to influence behavior from the unconscious mind (see Chapter 4).

Many people have heard stories of "hidden advertisements" which purportedly influence consumers without their awareness (e.g., messages of "drink Coke" flashed on movie screens too quickly to be detected). In fact, devices that play anti-shoplifting messages at unnoticably low levels are now being marketed (along with reports of dramatic reductions in theft). However, there is no scientific proof for the level of effectiveness their promoters often claim. Only under rather unusual conditions is there any evidence that we may be affected by subliminal stimuli. These conditions as identified by James McConnell (1983) are,

---

[1]. We are here discussing "absolute" thresholds. A "difference" threshold, also called a just noticeable difference" or j.n.d., is the minimum amount of change in stimulation necessary for the change to be detected.

First, you must be in a position where all the supra-liminal (above threshold) inputs available to you don't give you the information you need to make a decision. Second, you must be highly motivated to make use of even the weakest of "hunches." And third...there must be little or no cost to you for "guessing" at the correct answer. (241-42)

Basically, if you are forced to make a decision, which is of little consequence to you, and having no information on which to base your decision you decide to go with your feelings, you may be influenced by factors of which you are not aware. This is rather a weak basis for a science of "unconscious mind control," and the fears which the initial claims of subliminal perception generated, appear unwarranted. Nevertheless, reaction to stimuli not consciously perceived does appear possible (we will have more to say about "habits" of unconscious perception later when we discuss perceptual vigilance and defense).

Backmasking. Although the terms "masking," "backmasking," or "backwards masking" may have several meanings, we are using the term "backmasking" here in the popular sense to mean the backwards recording of messages on records or tapes so that when the record or tape is played, along with the regular music there is heard a message played backwards. When the record is played normally, the message is a garbled mixture of sounds indistinguishable from the background music. Only if the record is turned backwards on the turntable (potentially disastrous to the needle) is a message heard, and then only with great difficulty. Thus the message, or at least the sound of the message, is above the sensory threshold, but the message, in so far as it has any conscious meaning, is below the perceptual threshold.

Many people are not aware that this is sometimes done, and when it is brought to their attention it again brings fears of "unconscious mind control." This is particularly so among Christians, since the most common messages are apparently satanic ones placed on records of popular rock music groups (cf. "Charisma," April, 1983, 92-94). However, there is no scientific evidence for the effectiveness of backmasking. In a series of experiments

51

reported in the "American Psychologist" (1985, 40, 1231-1239), researchers John Vokey and Don Read found that subjects were not only unaffected by backwards messages, but were also unable even to decipher them. Furthermore, when subjects were given the idea that a certain message was present (as well-meaning religious leaders do in "exposing " backmasking), many of them reported hearing it-- even though it wasn't there!

Thus, as in the case of subliminal advertising discussed above, there is no scientific evidence that this procedure has any effect. Nevertheless, many Christians continue to fear unconscious (satanic) control. An interesting consequence is that some Christian artists have even used their own version of backmasking.

In summary, there is no significant evidence for what we have called "sensation without perception"; that is sensation and influence without conscious awareness. It does not appear that we are vulnerable to unconscious mind control either through stimuli presented at very weak levels or in an unusual (backwards) manner.

In a world where there are many blatant and very powerful negative influences (including far above-threshold satanic messages in popular music, not to mention the more subtle and alluring above-threshold messages so pervasive in mass advertising) Christians would do well to avoid "tilting at windmills" and the loss in credibility which fighting "unconscious mind control" would bring.

PERCEPTION WITHOUT SENSATION?

As indicated by the quotations which introduced this chapter, the subject of perception without sensation (more commonly known as "extra-sensory perception," or ESP), is potentially one of the more divisive issues with which we will deal.

Extra-sensory perception refers to the acquisition of information (perception) through means other than the normally identified senses (thus extra-sensory). It is usually divided into three categories:

52

1. If someone indicates (accurately) that he or she knows what you are thinking, without using normal channels of communication (including subtle nonverbal ones), thought transference or telepathy is said to be occurring.

2. If someone "knows" or "senses" (correctly) what is happening in another place which is out of earshot or eyesight, they are said to be clairvoyant.

3. If a person has a "feeling" that something will happen before it actually does, and they have no known reason for the feeling, they are said to experience precognition.

Many people will recognize that they have had experiences which fit these descriptions. Polls frequently show that not only do the majority of people believe in ESP but most people also claim to have personally experienced it. They may have "sensed" danger, had a "feeling in their bones," or "just knew" something. When asked for the basis of their knowledge they were unable to say. Sometimes these experiences are ascribed to "intuition" or a "sixth sense."

Christians commonly attribute similar experiences to the work of the Holy Spirit. They reason that God, having all knowledge, in His sovereignty may choose to reveal certain information to them concerning either the present (clairvoyance) or the future (precognition). If they put a label to it, they might call the former a "word of knowledge," the latter a "word of prophecy." Prayer can be regarded as a form of telepathy with God.

However, because Christians see a spiritual source for their own experiences (God), when non-Christians report similar experiences, many Christians are prone to identify the non-Christian's experience with demonic influence. Furthermore, not infrequently, spiritists have themselves claimed "extra-sensory" powers. Consequently, Christians are extremely wary of this "perception without sensation," relegating it to the shady regions of spiritism and the occult.

53

Most psychologists are very skeptical of ESP and thus it is relegated to parapsychology--literally "beyond" psychology. Many claims of ESP have been found to have other more traditional explanations. For example, "telepathy" has been shown in some cases to be the result of the reading of very subtle cues such as body language, or unconscious whispering, without either person being aware. And of course chance and trickery are difficult to rule out in ESP claims. Add to this the unreliability of ESP demonstrations and experiments and it is easy to see why psychologists are skeptical.[1]

On the one hand, then, we have our colleagues in psychology who are extremely skeptical that ESP even exists, and on the other hand our Christian brethren who believe in ESP but relegate it entirely to the spiritual realm as a communication from either God or demons. As Christians interested in psychology, how are we to find our way through this minefield of conflicting opinion? Is there sufficient room for a middle path which avoids triggering "mines" on either side--particularly the one labelled "biblical heresy"? It is not enough to reject ESP because it is difficult to demonstrate in the laboratory; prayer too is difficult to analyze scientifically. Neither should the many cases of trickery blind us to the possibility of something legitimate.

The most important issue for the Christian in psychology to work through is the biblical basis given by the detractors of ESP. As noted above a common argument for avoiding ESP is its association with the occult. Clearly, the Bible does warn against spiritism (e.g., Deut. 18:10-11), and spiritists often claim extra-sensory powers. However, this does not mean that anyone else having these powers receives them from spirits, or even that the spiritist himself does. A spiritist may use sleight of hand and claim that he or she is doing magic through the power of familiar spirits. This does not make sleight of hand wrong nor does it validate their claim to spirit influence. Sleight

---

1. For further discussion of subliminal stimulation see McConnell et al (1958); on trickery see Korem and Meier (1980); Randi (1980).

54

of hand is an ability which in itself is neither good nor bad (some Christian magicians use it to attract an audience and illustrate a Christian message). Perhaps ESP is a God-given ability which in itself is also morally neutral.

The guilt-by-association which ESP often suffers in the eyes of Christians is compounded by the use of terms which have connotations of spiritism-- terms such as "psychic" and "clairvoyant." More neutral terms such as "sixth sense" or "intuition" may help us view the subject more objectively. [1]

A second problem which some Christians have in accepting ESP is that they see it as a claim to be equal to God. Telepathy, clairvoyance, and precognition are abilities which God has and the fear is that in claiming these abilities ourselves we are claiming to be God. However, there is an important difference between claiming God-like abilities and claiming to be God. Even the most extreme claims of ESP fall far short of omniscience. Just as our intelligence, creativity, and rational thinking (which also are God-like traits) are only a shadow of God's abilities in these areas, so too any capacity for ESP which we may have would be expected to be merely a token of God's "ESP." In fact, it is because God has these abilities in their fullness, that Koteskey (1980) suggests that humans as the image of God may also have them in a weaker or partially obscured state.

The analogy with God certainly does not prove that humans have these abilities. They may in the end prove to be nothing more than chance, superstition and trickery. Or they may be found not to be morally neutral but the work of the Holy Spirit on one hand or demons on the other. In either case, clear and honest argument needs to brought to bear on the issue.

To summarize our discussion of the issue "How are Christians to evaluate claims of unusual

---

[1]. Christian novelist Madeleine L'Engle uses the old Irish word "kything" for what is here called mental telepathy.

perception?" we might make note of the following points:

1. We need to investigate as fully as possible the basis for claims made in the name of psychological science--are there valid studies supporting the claim or is it based on hearsay? A knowledge of research methods for the behavioral sciences is extremely valuable here.

2. We need to keep an open mind concerning the possibility of phenomena with which we are not acquainted--and which may even lie outside the realm of #1.

3. We need to have a clear idea of what the Scriptures do and do not teach.

Each of the topics discussed above, subliminal perception, backmasking, ESP, are ones which intrigue many contemporary Christians, not to mention many contemporary psychologists. They have been presented here in an attempt to stimulate further discussion. In order to keep that discussion focussed, a host of related issues has been ignored. We will turn now to some of these, outlining each in a briefer form. It is hoped that even this short introduction to these topics will provide a stimulus to further thought and investigation.

DISCUSSION QUESTIONS

Parapsychology. The term "parapsychology" is used as a broad reference to the study of phenomena considered to lie outside the realm of general psychology. ESP as discussed above is one such phenomenon. Other areas of interest to parapsychologists include "psychokinesis" (the mental manipulation of objects without touching them), "psychic healing" (unorthodox cures involving a "psychic" factor), "poltergeists" (ghosts which cause noise and disturbance), "discarnate survival" and "reincarnation."[1]

---

[1].　For example, see Wolman's "Handbook of Parapsychology" (1977).

56

As may be seen from this list the study of parapsychology shades very gradually into the study of the spirit world. It is no doubt unfortunate that such diverse phenomena are included under the same "umbrella," simply because they are not amenable to experimental verification. However, because of this connection, at least in terminology, Christians need to be very cautious in formulating their position on these topics. It may be that they are all to be avoided; it may be that they fall more legitimately within the sphere of theology (and/or demonology); or it may be that the Christian psychologist with a sound knowledge of Scripture and a commitment to the guidance of the Holy Spirit is the best equipped to explore them.

Although a Christian evaluation of parapsychology is not central to the relating of psychology and Christianity, it is becoming more urgent as interest in parapsychology continues to grow. The wide acceptance of ESP indicates the importance of establishing guidelines as to when "intuition" or "sixth sense" leaves off and when spiritism begins. Clear thinking on these issues is needed if the twin errors of premature rejection and naive acceptance are to be avoided.

Perceptual vigilance and defense. What little support there is for the effect of subliminal perception comes almost entirely from studies of perceptual vigilance and defense. These studies have shown that experimental subjects react to "smutty" or "taboo" words such as "whore" differently from neutral words such as "table." Some subjects take much longer to consciously recognize such words (perceptual defense), although physiological measures indicate that they are reacting to them unconsciously. Other subjects seem to be unconsciously looking for "smutty" words (perceptual vigilance), and recognize them sooner than neutral words (McGinnies, 1949; Bruner, 1957; Erdelyi, 1974).

These studies suggest that even at the unconscious level we have a fair amount of control over our perceptions. We are not such passive victims of the stimuli in our environment as we often think, but active programmers of our sensory world, responsible for the type of stimulation our minds receive. Studies of perceptual vigilance and defense suggest that even at the unconscious level we may be able to screen out unwanted stimuli.

Consideration of this area gives rise to some interesting questions for Christians in psychology. Are perceptual vigilance and defense the mechanisms by which our minds are "renewed" (Eph. 4:23)? Do they provide a scientific basis for Phillipians 4:8? That is, does "thinking on good things" establish unconscious perceptual mechanisms to build up and protect positive renewed minds?

Acupuncture. Acupuncture involves the insertion of needles at various points of the body in an attempt to reduce or eliminate pain. It is of interest to Christians because of its Eastern origins and the resultant speculation that spirits are involved. It is of interest to psychologists, and relevant here, because it involves a sometimes dramatic change in sensation--the elimination of pain (Mann et al, 1973).

With a gentle twisting motion, an acupuncturist inserts the ends of several 2 or 3 inch stainless steel needles at special points in the body (frequently the head, neck, and shoulders). Sometimes a mild electric current is passed through the needles. The needles themselves are not painful, but their effect is often to reduce or eliminate pain from other causes ranging from mild headaches to major surgical incisions.

There is no consensus as to the scientific basis for the effectiveness of acupuncture. It has been suggested that the needles trigger or open a "gate" in the pathway of the pain impulses so that they do not get through to the brain. On the other hand, or perhaps in addition, the needles and people's expectations may cause the body to release large amounts of its own pain-killing drug, endorphin (Mayer et al, 1976).

Is acupuncture an occult practice? Or is it a useful pain-killer with no harmful side-effects? Is there any reason for Christians to avoid acupuncture?

In conclusion, there are a variety of topics in the study of sensation and perception which are interesting and often controversial within the field of psychology itself. When they are viewed with specifically Christian assumptions in mind, further questions arise. Although some of the issues are perhaps not central to the relating of psychology and Christianity, discussion of them from a Christian perspective will inevitably aid in this process. Critical to the success of this process is a sound knowledge of Scripture, an openness to the unexpected, and a willingness to challenge what is widely accepted. It is hoped that the present chapter is a stimulus in this direction.

SUGGESTED READINGS

Koteskey, R.L. 1980. Psychology_from_a_Christian perspective. Nashville: Abingdon. Interesting in the context of this chapter for its openness to the study of parapsychological phenomena by Christians (pp. 73-74). Suggests these phenomena may be part of the image of God in humans.

Myers, D.G. 1983, July. ESP and the paranormal. Christianity_Today, 14-17. Good presentation of the traditional objections to parapsychological phenomena.

Vokey, J.R., & Read, J.D. (1985). Subliminal messages: Between the devil and the media. American_Psychologist, 40, 1231-1239. An excellent paper demonstrating some of the psychological processes behind the fear of subliminal influence. Mandatory reading for a discussion of backmasking.

REFERENCES AND OTHER SOURCES

Atkinson, R.L., Atkinson, R.C., & Hilgard, E.R. 1983. Introduction_to_psychology (8th ed.). New York: Harcourt Brace Jovanovich, Inc
Bolt, M., & Myers, D.G. 1984. The_human connection. Downers Grove, IL: InterVarsity Press.
Bruner, J.S. 1957. On perceptual readiness. Psychological_Review, 64, 123-152.

Coran, S., Porac, C., & Ward, L. 1984. Sensation and perception (2nd ed.). New York: Academic Press.

Erdelyi, M.H. 1974. A new look at the New Look: Perceptual defense and vigilance. Psychological Review, 81, 1-25.

Evangelists warn of hidden rock-n-roll messages. 1983, April. Charisma, 92-94.

Henley, S.H. 1984. A comment on Merikle's 1982 paper. Bulletin of the Psychonomic Society, 22, 121-124.

Korem, D., & Meier, P. 1980. The fakers. Grand Rapids: Baker.

Koteskey, R.L. 1980. Psychology from a Christian perspective. Nashville: Abingdon.

Mann, F., Bowsher, D., Mumford, J., Lipton, S., & Miles, J. 1973. Treatment of intractable pain by acupuncture. Lancet, 2, 57-60.

Mayer, D.J., Price, D.D., Rafii, A., & Barber, J. 1976. Acupuncture hypalgesia: Evidence for activation of a central control system as a mechanism of action. In Bonica, J.J., & Albe-Fessard, D., Eds., Advances in pain research and therapy, vol. 1 New York: Ravens Press.

McConnell, J.V. 1983. Understanding human behavior (4th ed.). New York: Holt, Rinehart and Winston.

McGinnies, E. 1949. Emotionality and perceptual defense. Psychological Review, 56, 244-251.

Merikle, P.M. 1982. Unconscious perception revisited. Perception and Psychophysics, 31, 298-301.

Myers, D.G. 1983, July. ESP and the paranormal. Christianity Today, 14-17.

Vokey, J.R., & Read, J.D. (1985). Subliminal messages: Between the devil and the media. American Psychologist, 40, 1231-1239.

Wolman, B.B., ed. 1977. Handbook of parapsychology. New York; Van Nostrand Reinhold Company.

> Do we have an unconscious mind which plays a role in Christian experience?

WHAT IS CONSCIOUSNESS?
THE UNCONSCIOUS MIND
CONTROVERSIAL ISSUE
    No significant unconscious mind
    Unconscious mind important
DISCUSSION QUESTIONS
    Dreams
    Hypnosis
    Meditation
    Mystical states, drugs, and other levels
    Archetypes
SUGGESTED READINGS
REFERENCES AND OTHER SOURCES

Are you conscious? "Of course," you say, "I couldn't read this page without being conscious." But how conscious are you? Are you completely aware of all the stimuli that are influencing you at this moment? Are you even aware of all the stimuli from within your own mind that are influencing you?

Do we have an **unconscious mind** which plays a role in Christian experience?

We will see that our discussion of this issue has possible implications for our understanding of a variety of religious experiences, including conversion, prayer, glossolalia, and sanctification. We will also be raising for discussion the question of a Christian attitude to dreams, hypnosis, meditation, drugs, and mystical states.

However, before we can consider these controversial topics we must define some terms and explain some concepts.

WHAT IS CONSCIOUSNESS?

Consciousness is generally synonymous with awareness. It includes our awareness of our thoughts, feelings, and memories, as well as our perceptions of the world around us. Obviously this changes from moment to moment. One moment we are alert, straining every nerve to perceive whether or not there is an intruder in our home; the next moment we sink into our thoughts, almost oblivious to our surroundings; later we drift off to sleep and our awareness shifts to the fantastic world of dreams. If we take certain drugs, practice meditation, or undergo hypnosis we will experience still other states of consciousness. However, most of us have a "normal state" in which we spend the bulk of our waking hours.

One of the most intriguing questions regarding consciousness is the degree to which the various states may affect one another (e.g., waking and dream states) and the possibility that they all may be affected by or even determined by a deeper level of consciousness of which we are unaware-- the so-called subconscious or unconscious mind.

THE UNCONSCIOUS MIND

Although discussion of unconscious mental events may be traced to Fechner (1801-1887), Herbart (1776-1841), Leibnitz (1646-1716) and even to Plato, it was Sigmund Freud who brought the subject to prominence in psychology at the beginning of this century. Drawing upon an analogy suggested by Fechner, Freud likened the mind to an iceberg in which only about one tenth is accessible to consciousness and conscious influences. The remaining nine tenths is driven by strong unconscious currents and is inaccessible to conscious awareness.

Actually Freud distinguished three levels of consciousness: the conscious, the preconscious, and the unconscious. The conscious level includes all the sensations and perceptions of which we are actually aware at the moment. The preconscious level is the level of available memory; that is, all the experiences which, although not conscious at the moment, could readily or with a minimum of effort, be brought to conscious awareness. This might include such things as what you were doing an hour ago, or your postal code, etc.

The deepest and most significant level of the mind is the unconscious level, or simply the unconscious. The significance of this level lies in the fact that although we are not aware of its contents, or even its existence, it is the primary determinant of our behavior. Freud asserted that most of our behavior, and certainly all of our important behavior was shaped and directed by impulses, conflicts, and drives completely beyond our awareness. The unconscious is a bubbling cauldron of memories and impulses which are too threatening to admit to awareness, and consequently are pushed down, or **repressed** into the unconscious. This includes thoughts of anger, hate, aggression, and lust, as well as the two basic drives to life ("eros"), and death ("thanatos"). The primary source of these thoughts (especially those of sex and aggression) is the biological component of the personality which Freud called the **id**. But the **superego**, comprised of the internalized goals and restrictions of society, also acts at this level, as does the rational mediator, the **ego**. Hence, there is continual conflict within the personality at this unconscious level. The id wants immediate gratification of its drives, the superego tries to substitute moralistic goals for the id's selfish ones, and the ego attempts to mediate among the id, the superego, and objective reality. Thus the unconscious contains not only the memories of events which are too unpleasant to recall, but also an ongoing conflict, or at best an uneasy truce, between id, ego, and superego. Freud's method of therapy, psychoanalysis, was directed at bringing to awareness these unconscious processes and helping the ego to deal with them in a rational way.

The effect of unconscious processes is seen most clearly in dreams, which Freud called the "royal road to the unconscious." Dreams are a disguised expression of the unconscious. Freud felt that the careful interpretation of dreams would reveal important sources of unconscious motivation. Unconscious motivation is also revealed in all manner of errors of writing and speaking ("slips of tongue," or "Freudian slips"), as well as through "free association" (i.e., saying whatever comes to mind), and hypnosis.

Carl Jung, who for a time was associated with Freud, developed his own theory of personality in which he proposed a further unconscious system which he called the "collective unconscious." Whereas the "personal unconscious" as described by Freud contains repressed memories of personal experiences, the collective unconscious contains the residue of certain experiences common to the human race. The residue of these experiences is passed on from generation to generation over thousands of years and gradually builds up a kind of framework (or "archetype") around which subsequent personal experiences are organized. Jung suggested, for example, that we have archetypes of power, of God, and of demons. It takes very little personal experience before we arrive at these concepts ourselves, even if our culture didn't teach them to us.

In summary, then, there is a long history of suggestion that we are affected by mental events of which we are not entirely aware. This concept formed the basis of an elaborate theory of personality proposed by Sigmund Freud. Freud felt that most of our behavior was directed by drives and impulses arising from memories and conflicts in a part of our mind which he called the unconscious. This unconscious is inaccessible to awareness except through extraordinary means such as hypnosis, and psychoanalysis, including dream analysis. Carl Jung has further suggested that we may be affected by unconscious archetypes inherited from our racial ancestors. Both men felt that we ignore our unconscious minds at our peril.

CONTROVERSIAL ISSUE

Jung's idea of a collective unconscious, although based on evidence from a wide variety of cultures, religions, and times, is very controversial and far from universally accepted. Freud's view too has been widely criticized. Let us look at some of this negative reaction and then consider the implications of these concepts for a Christian view of the person. For certainly one of the fundamental issues which a Christian view of the person must deal with is the question of the extent to which the person is controlled by events of which they are not aware and over which they have no control.

No significant unconscious mind. Although Freud's view of unconscious motivation had a significant impact on the thinking of his day, it was not long before differing viewpoints were heard. Even one of Freud's early followers, Alfred Adler, felt that conscious social factors were more important than the unconscious, predominantly sexual factors Freud identified. However it was the force of Behaviorism sweeping across North America in the second and third decades of this century which presented the most influential challenge to the concept of unconscious motivation.

When John Watson published his paper "Psychology as the Behaviorist Views It" in 1913, he said, "What we need to do is to start work upon psychology, making **behavior**, not **consciousness**, the objective point of our attack." In rejecting consciousness, at all levels, Watson was rejecting all mentalistic concepts invoked to explain behavior. His arguments were straightforward. No one has ever seen or measured a "consciousness" (much less an unconscious), a mind, or any other supposed mental structure or event. Speculation about these hypothetical constructs is futile and only leads to confusion. Therefore we must restrict our discussion to observations upon which we can agree. We will study behavior--nothing else. Watson's ideas were seen as "a breath of fresh air, clearing away the musty accumulation of the centuries" (R.I. Watson, 1978, 461). It was an idea which was right for the times and behaviorism became the dominant force in psychology for aproximately 50 years.

Behaviorism is carried to its logical conclusion in the work of B.F. Skinner who has been called "the most influential psychologist of our time" (Hjelle and Zeigler, 1981, 189). Skinner has developed a complete approach to human behavior relying exclusively on observable antecedent conditions, behavior, and its consequences, without resource to mentalistic concepts either conscious or unconscious. Furthermore, an effective behavioristic approach to psychotherapy (called behavior therapy), has been developed. This approach treats disorders as problems in behavior without regard to any supposed underlying causes such as unconscious conflicts. Behaviorism thus appears to have shown that the unconscious is at best an unnecessary concept.

But what of the evidence upon which Freud built his theories? What of the subjective mental experience of consciousness? And what of dreams?

From a behaviorist point of view these things are merely incidental to behavior--a kind of sideshow to the main event. They may go along with behavior but they do not determine it, and thus are of little consequence.

Neurophysiology has also weakened the case for a significant unconscious. Hobson and McCarley, for example, propose that we think of dreaming as the psychological concommitant of an essentially biological process (cf. McCarley, 1978). They suggest that at various times during sleep certain brain cells in the lower centers become activated and that on the basis of stored memories and past experiences the higher brain or cortex tries to make sense out of this meaningless stimulation. The result is the disjointed, often bizarre experience we call a dream. Francis Crick and Graeme Mitchison, on the other hand, have proposed that dreams may be the brain's way of wiping out false or nonsensical memories--a kind of neural housecleaning (cf. Melnechuk, 1983). The process may be likened to "unlearning" or "reverse learning" in which useless and potentially interfering neural networks are erased-- "We dream in order to forget our dreams." Most often we do not remember our dreams when we wake; if we do, the process must be gone through again. In either case dreams are not the expression of a powerful unconscious mind, and they have no inherent meaning.

Koster (1984) has suggested that perhaps the conceptual distinction between a conscious and an unconscious mind merely reflects different functions of the two hemispheres or halves of the brain (specifically the cerebral cortex). Generally speaking, the left, or dominant hemisphere is specialized for dealing with verbal tasks, and the right hemisphere for spatial, intuitive, non-verbal tasks. Perhaps the effect of this division of labor is to create the illusion of separate conscious and unconscious minds.

Let us consider what might be happening in the case of hypnosis, one of the favorite evidences for the existence of an unconscious mind.

In order to limit severe epileptic seizures patients sometimes have the right and left halves of their brains (cortex) separated so that the two halves cannot communicate with each other. This is accomplished by severing the connecting tissue called the corpus callosum. Each half still receives input and sends messages to control behavior. Speech and other verbal behavior is carried on, as before, in the left hemisphere, with the right hemisphere continuing to process spatial, primarily nonverbal material. The major difference is that these two functions are not integrated within the split brain. Because communication between halves is not possible, if a message is sent to one side only, the other may have no explanation for the behavior which follows. For example, if the right hemisphere (usually predominantly nonverbal) is given a message to pick up a certain object, the left hand, which is controlled by the right hemisphere, may move to the correct object and pick it up. However, when the subject is asked why he or she did this, the message will be received, processed and responded to from the left (verbal) hemisphere which had no knowledge of the message to the right hemisphere. The left hemisphere will respond by fabricating a reason for the behavior.

This situation bears a remarkable similarity to certain behaviors resulting from hypnosis, particularly post-hypnotic suggestion. For example, subjects under hypnosis may be told that after they awake from the hypnotic state, at a certain signal, perhaps the hypnotist coughing, they will pick up a particular object, and moreover, will not remember that they had been told to do this. When the subjects are out of the hypnotic state, and the hypnotist coughs, they will feel compelled to pick up the object. When asked why they are doing this they apparently do not remember the hypnotic suggestion, and will fabricate a reason for their behavior.

The similarity of these two phenomena suggests an explanation of the second in terms of the first. Perhaps hypnosis involves the "splitting off" of the left hemisphere so that it is idle (asleep?) while the right hemisphere remains conscious.[1] The post-hypnotic suggestion is stored in the right hemisphere only (as with the split-brain subject) so that later when the appropriate stimulus is received it evokes the pre-arranged response from

---

[1]. While the right hemisphere is predominantly nonverbal, it has some limited verbal ability--for all its specialization the brain is remarkably redundant. It may be noted that verbal ability, especially responsiveness, is greatly reduced under hypnosis.

the right hemisphere and nothing from the left. The command that the source of the suggestion not be remembered may merely prevent the communication of this information to the left hemisphere.

Perhaps when hypnotists speak of relaxing, putting aside all disturbing thoughts, and going deeper and deeper into the unconscious mind, we may think of laying aside, lulling to sleep, or "splitting off," the left, or verbal hemisphere, and becoming more and more aware of processes in the right hemisphere.[1] Whereas the left hemisphere is responsible for logical, sequential, verbal behavior, the right hemisphere operates intuitively, with images, and in a parallel, or non-sequential manner. This distinction is not unlike that between the conscious and unconscious minds, the conscious mind being rational, reality orientated, and communicative, the unconscious being irrational, intuitive, and largely non-verbal.

This is not to say that all functions in the right hemisphere are unconscious; obviously they are not. Right hemisphere functioning is the basis for spatial and geometric ability, for example, which is just as conscious as purely verbal functioning. However, perhaps the result of having one hemisphere of the brain which operates on an intuitive, non-verbal level simultaneously with the more communicative left hemisphere, is to feel as though there is some part of the self which is not available to consciousness--a kind of ghost or shadow personality--an unconscious mind.

The verbal emphasis in Western culture, and particularly in adults, magnifies the importance of left hemisphere functions to the point that right hemisphere functions seem secondary, shadowy and "other." Again the similarity between the theoretical constructs of normal conscious/unconscious minds and the exaggerrated effects of left and right hemisphere "personalities" in split-brain subjects may be revealing.

_____

[1]. A similar description could be given for meditation as a form of unguided hypnosis.

Thus the existence of an unconscious mind of any great significance is by no means universally accepted. We may note the following relevant points:

1. Adler, and many others after him, have pointed to other motivational influences as being far more significant than those arising from the unconscious.

2. Behaviorists, notably Watson and Skinner, have developed a thorough analysis of human behavior, including numerous practical applications, without recourse to the concept of an unconscious mind.

3. Neurophysiological explanations exist for most, if not all, of the phenomena usually attributed to an unconscious mind. As noted in Chapter 1 these explanations are merely on another "level" and do not necessarily disprove other explanations. However, if correct, they probably necessitate at least serious modification to the traditional view since there is no reason to believe the right hemisphere, as the possible origin of unconscious phenomena, is the primary basis of repressed instincts, conflicts, or memories. In the end the more parsimonious "nothing but physiology" view may be adequate and even preferable as an explanation of phenomena attributed to the unconscious.

Christians have some additional reasons to be skeptical of Freud's view of the unconscious. Objections they might raise include the following:

1. Since we probably assume that God does not have an unconscious mind, if He created humans with one it is certainly a significant way in which His image is not reflected in humans.

2. Would God hold humans responsible for their behavior if it is primarily motivated by an unconscious mind over which they have virtually no control?

3. Jesus was "tempted in all points like as we are, yet without sin." Did He have an unconscious

mind full of repressed memories and sexual conflicts? (Did Adam? Will we after death?)

These then are some of the arguments against the Freudian concept of an unconscious mind. They come not only from secular psychology but also from specifically Christian concerns.

Unconscious mind important. Despite the objections noted above, perhaps through ignorance of them, it is my experience that most people, including most Christians, believe in some form of unconscious motivation. They frequently use the term unconscious or subconscious in their everyday speech, and when asked directly readily admit that they believe in some form of unconscious motivation. However, when called upon to relate their views of the unconscious to some of the objections noted above and to the phenomena of dreams, hypnosis, and meditation, they are at a loss. Is it possible to answer the objections, giving an affirmative answer to our "controversial issue," and in so doing develop a Christian view of the unconscious? Such a view could have broad implications for the understanding of Christian experience as well as providing a valuable contribution to the "integrative" process--the relating of psychology and Christianity.

Recently several steps have been taken to re-interpret Freudian concepts in a Christian context.[1] Vitz and Gartner see their work as a kind of "Christianized psychoanalysis" and further state "...even at this stage we are willing to suggest that a fully developed Christian interpretation of psychoanalysis appears possible" (1984b, 89).

Given the central role of the unconscious in psychoanalytic thought, a "fully developed Christian interpretation of psychoanalysis" will surely include a Christian view of the unconscious

---

[1]. Some examples of Christian interpretations of psychoanalytic concepts are: Shepperson, 1981, Shepperson and Henslin, 1984, on hypnosis; Vitz and Gartner, 1984a "Jesus as the Anti-Oedipus," and 1984b "Jesus the Transformer of the Super-Ego."

(not to mention a Christian interpretation of dreams, and possible Christian uses of hypnosis). But what will a Christian view of the unconscious look like?

The following assumptions would seem to be the minimal basis upon which any theory of the unconscious could be based:

1. People have within them the capacity to retain a great deal more than they normally recognize, perhaps **all** their experience (although probably not the vast array of sensory bombardment which does not pass the sensory storage stage of memory).

2. Not all of this retained material is available to consciousness.

3. Retained but unavailable material may affect mental processes and behavior.

In its simplest form this position agrees with traditional psychoanalytic theory that an unconscious mind exists and influences behavior. We need not conclude that all or even most motivation from the unconscious is sexual. Neither is it necessarily immoral, although existing in fallen men and women as it does it is definitely inclined this way. In fact we may view the unconscious as being comprised of nothing more nor less than all those memories and feelings which we cannot, under normal circumstances, bring to awareness (this may or may not include **all** of a person's experience). Many memories may be beyond normal recall because of the unpleasant emotion associated with them. In psychoanalytic terms they are repressed. The same may be true for many "unacceptable" urges or instincts. However, there may also be material below the level of conscious awareness which is beyond recall for more mundane reasons; similar memories occurring either before or after the target memories may interfere with their recall to conscious memory.

In the traditional Freudian psychoanalytic view a child is born as a bundle of unconscious instincts from which a relatively insignificant consciousness only gradually emerges. This consciousness remains heavily influenced by unconscious forces. Recent trends in psychoanalytic theory have placed greater emphasis on conscious forces in the personality, especially the "ego" (Erikson, Hartmann, Kris, Murray). In fact we may go further and see the conscious self as primary, with the unconscious being **formed** as the individual struggles to hide unacceptable motives from the conscious self or ego. A view of the unconscious being formed from previously conscious material would seem to be necessary to allow for individual responsibility for motivation arising from the unconscious (see our "Christian objection" #2 above).

If the unconscious is the psychic reservoir for fears, failures, lust, etc., which are repressed through our unfortunate inability to deal with them, then the influence from this reservoir is ultimately our own responsibility. It follows that had we faced our fears, not failed, or lusted, we would not have to deal with negative influences from the unconscious. This, no doubt, was our Lord's situation (and Adam's before the fall, as well as ours ultimately). Furthermore, if having sinned, we confess our failure and ask forgiveness, repression of the incident becomes unnecessary.

A biblical view of the person clearly assumes that, whether or not he or she is aware of their own sources of motivation, God is aware (Heb. 4:12). Humans are completely open before God-- whether they know it or not, and whether they wish it or not. A Christian view of the unconscious thus will go beyond what Koteskey (1980) has called the "animal-like" characteristics of humans, the biological drives and instincts which Freud said determined so much of our behavior. A Christian view of the unconscious will allow for the Holy Spirit to work even at this level, redeeming our fallen nature.

If then humans have a part of their psyche which to them is unconscious but nevertheless is open to God, the question arises, how does the unconscious influence or enter into the relationship between them and God? For example, how might the unconscious enter into the experience of conversion?

A psychoanalytic interpretation might suggest that conversion is the result of unconscious sexual conflicts which cause great anxiety as they seek to become conscious. Conversion reduces the anxiety by redirecting ("displacing" or "sublimating") psychic ("libidinal") energy toward God. Various elaborations and variations of this description may be offered from a psychodynamic point of view (e.g., conversion as resolution of a renewed oedipal conflict (Freud, 1928)). The common factor is the important (determining) role of unconscious forces. However, the observation that unconscious factors may be involved need not lead to the conclusion that they are decisive on their own. As Johnson and Malony point out, "Christian conversion may coincide with a state of conflict which is part of both the conscious and unconscious experience of the person" (1982, 52). Unconscious influences may be a factor just as sociological influences (cf. Lofland and Stark, 1965) are a factor. The role of the Holy Spirit in the unconscious mind of an unregenerate person deserves further study. Perhaps the unconscious struggle is largely the work of the Holy Spirit, or perhaps He is prevented from working at this level until the conscious faculty of will is yielded.

It is more obvious that the Holy Spirit is working in the unconscious mind of the believer "conforming him to the image of the likeness of Christ." Groeschel (1984) has presented a psychological analysis of spiritual development which sees as a significant part of this development the release of defense mechanisms (e.g., repression, denial), and a complete openness to God.[1] Citing Meister Eckhart, he says,

> The essence of the psychological process of union with God is not awareness of God, but rather the openness of the mind and will to God--undisturbed by contradictory desires, hidden goals, and unresolved conflicts, and

---

[1]. Defense mechanisms are psychological processes or "manipulations" we go through in order to protect our conscious thoughts from some unacceptable motive or urge from within. A very familiar one is rationalization.

open to reality on all levels because of the relinquishment of defense mechanisms and other unrealistic behavior. (165)

This process may involve many apparent setbacks as old battles with the flesh (id, libido) emerge when familiar defenses are given up. The way is arduous and long, usually not completed in a life-time. However, the process produces significant psychological change:

Psychologically one may speculate that all defenses have now been reduced to practically nothing and that one is dealing with a human being who appears to have been healed of the wounds of original sin. (179)

Although from somewhat different perspectives, John Sanford (1970), and M. Scott Peck (1978) also view spiritual growth as a process of becoming aware of the unconscious.

"Inner healing" or "healing of memories" (advocated by Seamands, 1981, 1985, Stapleton, 1976, and severely criticized by Hunt and McMahon, 1985) would seem to involve similar processes, although in a more restricted or concentrated way. Defense mechanisms such as repression, denial, projection, are given up as the Holy Spirit guides the individual to harmful memories (repressed) and enables him to forgive those who have wronged him.

Prayer too may involve deep unconscious processes, as Ann and Barry Ulanov have noted (1982). Even the phenomena of glossolalia ("speaking in tongues") may have its roots in the work of the Holy Spirit at the unconscious level.

At conversion the individual receives the Holy Spirit, is baptized by the Spirit into the Body of Christ. At this time the Holy Spirit begins to work within the individual (or work more freely) at the unconscious level. The goal of this process is complete openness to God and submission to the Holy Spirit. The experience identified by charismatics as a "baptism of the Holy Spirit" may represent an overflow from the unconscious of the presence of the Holy Spirit, who was resident within the believer from conversion but at this moment encounters less resistance from the conscious mind and controls him in a more complete way. [1]

The Holy Spirit may be very active at the unconscious level. In this view the process of conviction may be seen at least partly as a growing awareness of an "unconscious God" (cf. Frankl, 1975); conversion may be among other things, admitting to awareness this unconscious spirituality; sanctification may be at least partially the gradual removal of psychological defenses so that previously repressed instincts, motives, and conflicts are brought to awareness and dealt with; and prayer, perhaps even glossolalia, may have significant repercussions in the unconscious mind.

This point of view, of course, is highly speculative. Nevertheless, the concept of an unconscious mind may prove to be a valuable integrative concept underlying a variety of religious experiences.

DISCUSSION QUESTIONS

The following issues continue to be controversial. They are presented here in brief form in order to encourage further discussion. Of course the position taken on these issues will be affected by the position taken on the main issue of the existence on an unconscious mind and its relationship to God.

Dreams. Most people ignore their dreams. The majority of psychologists consider the analysis of dreams to be at best, highly speculative. However, dreams are often of great significance in the Bible. Moreover, some Christian psychologists consider dreams to be the voice of God speaking to us in the "language of the soul"

---

[1].   If, as we speculated earlier, the right cerebral hemisphere can be identified with the unconscious, the effect of glossolalia may be to occupy the left, or verbal hemisphere, so that it no longer inhibits the right hemisphere. The significance thus may be not so much in the vocalization as in the greater freedom which it allows the unconscious mind.

(Sanford, 1968, 1978; Savary et al, 1984; Schmitt, 1984). Can we listen to God speak to us through our dreams? Do we need a Christian theory of dream interpretation?

Hypnosis. Many Christians are wary of hypnosis because of the loss of control they associate with it, or because they fear it will leave them open to demonic influence (Bobgan and Bobgan, 1984; Hunt and McMahon, 1985; Nee, 1972). However, many psychologists think it is just another example of the mind's ability to separate or "dissociate" itself from the immediate environment, similar to many people's experience of "highway hypnosis." Perhaps it is nothing more than "guided meditation." Some Christians find it a useful tool in therapy (e.g., Shepperson, 1981; Shepperson and Henslin, 1984). Can hypnosis be useful to Christians?

Meditation. The Bible encourages Christians to meditate on God's Word (e.g., Josh. 1:8; Ps. 1:2; I Tim. 4:15). Many psychologists advocate relaxation and meditation training for mental health and personal development. Are they pushing Eastern religions? Is meditation necessarily religious? What is the value of meditation for Christians?

Mystical states, drugs, and other levels. While dreaming we are not usually aware of a waking state of consciousness. Everything we experience seems real and natural in the dream. Another level of consciousness (i.e., being awake) does not even occur to us as a possibility.

However, when we wake, we are immediately aware of the peculiarities of dream consciousness. We conclude that however "real" events seemed when we dreamed, they are less real than the events we experience while awake. We may even affirm that only those events in waking consciousness have any claim to reality at all. We base this conclusion at least partly on the apparent similarity of our waking experiences with those of other people in the same situation. In contrast, no one even observes our dreams, much less is aware of their participation in them. Thus these two states of consciousness are readily distinguished (those who are unable to do so are

77

experiencing hallucinations, and are generally considered abnormal). Because events in waking consciousness are considered more "real" and because waking consciousness includes awareness of dream consciousness (except for simple memory failures), but not vice versa, we consider waking consciousness a "higher" more inclusive level of consciousness.

If there exist higher levels of consciousness than waking consciousness, they should include at least these two characteristics :

1. Events or experiences at this level should appear at least as "real," and, in comparison to waking consciousness from these "higher" perspectives, probably more real (perhaps including greater certainty of the shared nature of the experience).

2. Higher levels should be inclusive of lower forms of consciousness (i.e., there should be an awareness of lower forms of consciousness). Like dream consciousness we would not consider it higher if we were aware of only that state.

Mystical states may represent such a level of consciousness. Mystics report a feeling of "oneness" with God, humankind, and/or the universe which indicate a deeper "shared experience" i.e., with all that is. They report being in touch with true reality (cf. Maslow, 1964; Stace, 1960). Their difficulty in describing their experience (its ineffability) may be a result of trying to describe a "higher" state while in a "lower" one (one would not expect to describe wakefulness to someone in one's dream).

By extrapolation, we may further speculate that should self awareness or consciousness survive physical death, in a "resurrected" or "glorified" body, it would probably be of this "higher" sort, perhaps like that of mystical experiences, perhaps higher yet. It should include knowledge of present happenings, seen from a new "truer" perspective (as dreams are seen in "true" perspective after awaking). It would also involve a more full and inclusive experience of reality-- possibly as different from waking consciousness as waking consciousness is from dreaming. It will mean waking to a new reality with full knowledge of all previous perspectives together with an understanding of their inadequacies and limitations.

Are mystical states a higher level of consciousness? (Are dreams a lower level of consciousness?)

Should Christians use drugs to attain or enhance mystical states of religious experience as they have used fasting and prolonged isolation?[1]

Archetypes. Humans were created in the image of God with a much expanded awareness, including an awareness of God, with whom they communicated daily. However, attaining to greater wisdom, they fell, and their "foolish heart was darkened" (Rom. 1:21). The result was not only a loss in direct communion with God but even a diminished awareness of God--God became what Frankl (1975) has called the "unconscious God" (or God perceived by a spiritually sensitive unconscious).

Is this diminished awareness a "God archetype" (Jung)?

Is the archetype of God what the Bible is referring to when it says that God has "set eternity in their hearts" (Eccl. 3:11), so that "that which is known about God is evident within them; for God made it evident to them" (Rom. 1:19)?

Is Pascal's "God-shaped vacuum" Jung's archetype?

In conclusion, we have seen that the concept of an unconscious mind has both a long history as well as a significant amount of popular acceptance. However, among psychologists it is far from universally accepted, especially in its original form as proposed by Freud. After a brief description of the concept we examined some

---

[1]. For a discussion of the relationship between physiology and religious experience see Chapter 2; also Clark, Malony, Daane, and Tippett, 1973, on drugs.

arguments against its value. We then considered what Christians might consider an acceptable modification of Freud's original concept, and noted some implications for specific religious experience. Finally, some questions for further discussion were noted briefly.

It is hoped that both the discussion here and the questions raised will prove germane to the further development of this important aspect of Christian psychology.

SUGGESTED READINGS

Bobgan, M., & Bobgan, D. 1984. Hypnosis and the Christian. Minneapolis: Bethany House. Criticism of hypnosis from a Christian point of view. Cites possible harmful effects and uses the Bible to justify the complete rejection o f hypnosis.

Clark, W.H., Malony, H.N., Daane, J., & Tippett, A.R. 1973. Religious experience: Its nature and function in the human psyche. Springfield: Charles Thomas. Included is an interesting debate on the role of drugs in religious experience.

Johnson, C.B., & Malony, H.N. 1982. Christian conversion: Biblical and psychological perspectives. Grand Rapids, MI: Zondervan. Thorough, readable analysis of conversion from psychological and biblical perspectives. Good discussion of the problems in studying religious experience.

Groeschel, B.J. 1984. Spiritual passages: The psychology of spiritual development. New York: Crossroad. Contains many helpful insights on psychological processes which may accompany spiritual growth. Written from a classical religious perspective.

McCarley, R.W. 1978, December. "Where dreams come from: A new theory." Psychology Today, 53-141. Interesting discussion of the parallels between neuronal activity and dream experience. Suggests dreams have rather obvious undisguised meaning.

Schmitt, A. 1984. Before I wake. Nashville: Abingdon. Arguments and evidence for God speaking through dreams today. Includes some suggestions on how to listen to dreams. For the layman.

Shepperson, V.L., & Henslin, E.R. 1984. "Hypnosis and metaphor in Christian context: History, abuse, and use." Journal of Psychology and Theology, 12, 100-108. Helpful discussion of the use of hypnosis by Christians. Considers the fears which many Christians have about the subject. Describes one technique of hypnosis (see also Shepperson, 1981).

Springer, S.P., & Deutsch, G. 1985. Left brain, right brain. (2nd ed.) New York: Freeman. Probably the most accepted standard reference in the field of left and right brain differences.

REFERENCES AND OTHER SOURCES

Bobgan, M., & Bobgan, D. 1984. Hypnosis and the Christian. Minneapolis: Bethany House.

Clark, W.H., Malony, H.N., Daane, J., & Tippett, A.R. 1973. Religious experience: Its nature and function in the human psyche. Springfield: Charles Thomas.

Frankl, V.E. 1975. The unconscious God. New York: Simon and Schuster.

Freud, S. 1928. A religious experience. In James Strachey (Ed. & Trans.), The standard edition of the complete psychological works of Sigmund Freud (Vol. 21). London: Hogarth, 1961.

Groeschel, B.J. 1984. Spiritual passages: The psychology of spiritual development. New York: Crossroad.

Guntrip, H. 1971. The ego psychology of Freud and Adler re-examined in the 1970s. British Journal of Medical Psychology, 44, 305-318.

Hjelle, L.A. & Ziegler, D.J. 1981. Personality theories: Basic assumptions, research, and applications. New York: McGraw-Hill.

McCarley, R.W. 1978, December. "Where dreams come from: A new theory." Psychology Today, 53-141.

Melnechuk, T. 1983, November. "The dream machine." Psychology Today, 22.

Johnson, C.B., & Malony, H.N. 1982. Christian conversion: Biblical and psychological perspectives. Grand Rapids, MI: Zondervan.

Kelsey, M.T. 1974. God, dreams, and revelation. Minneapolis: Augsburg.

Koster, E. W. 1984. Testing the spirits. Journal of Psychology and Christianity, 3, 35-43.

Koteskey, R.L. 1980. Psychology from a Christian perspective. Nashville: Abingdon.

Lofland, J., & Stark, R. 1965. "Becoming a world saver: A theory of conversion to a deviant perspective." American Sociological Review, 30, 862-875.

Martin, D., & Mullen, P. 1984. Strange gifts: A guide to charismatic renewal. New York: Basil Blackwell.

Maslow, A. 1964. Religions, values, and peak-experiences. New York: The Viking Press.

Nee, W. 1972. The latent power of the soul. New York: Christian Fellowship.

Peck, M.S. 1978. The road less travelled. New York: Simon and Schuster.

Sanford, J.A. 1968. Dreams: God's forgotten language. New York: Harper and Row.

Sanford, J.A. 1970. The kingdom within. New York: Paulist Press.

Sanford, J.A. 1978. Dreams and healing. New York: Paulist Press.

Savary, L.M., Berne, P.H., & Williams, S.K. 1984. Dreams and spiritual growth: A Christian approach to dreamwork. New York: Paulist Press.

Schmitt, A. 1984. Before I wake. Nashville: Abingdon.

Seamands, D.A. 1981. Healing for damaged emotions. Wheaton, IL: Victor Books.

Seamands, D.A. 1985. Healing of memories. Wheaton, IL: Victor Books.

Shepperson, V.L. 1981. Paradox, parables, and change: One approach to Christian hypnotherapy. Journal of Psychology and Theology, 9, 3-11.

Shepperson, V.L., & Henslin, E.R. 1984. Hypnosis and metaphor in Christian context: History, abuse, and use. Journal of Psychology and Theology, 12, 100-108.

Springer, S.P., & Deutsch, G. 1985. Left brain, right brain. (2nd ed.) New York: Freeman.

Stace, W.T. 1960. Mysticism and philosophy. Philadelphia: Lippincott.

Stapleton, R.C. 1976. The gift of inner healing. Waco, TX: Word.

Ulanov, A., & Ulanov, B. 1982. Primary speech: A psychology of prayer. Atlanta: John Knox.

Vitz, P.C., & Gartner, J.G. 1984. "Christianity and psychoanalysis, part 1: Jesus as the anti-Oedipus." Journal of Psychology and Theology, 12, 4-14.

Vitz, P.C., & Gartner, J.G. 1984. Christianity and psychoanalysis, part 2: Jesus the transformer of the super-ego. Journal of Psychology and Theology, 12, 82-90.

Walsh, J.A. 1983. The dream of Joseph: A Jungian interpretation. Journal of Psychology and Theology, 11, 20-27.

Watson, John B. 1913. Psychology as the behaviorist views it. Psychological Review, 20, 158-177.

Watson, R.I. 1978. The great psychologists, (4th ed.). Philadelphia: Lippincott.

CHAPTER 5: DEVELOPMENTAL PSYCHOLOGY

Can developmental psychology aid in the understanding of religious development?

85

With drool running down her chin and intense concentration in every move, she leaned forward and reached out her chubby hand. Although the first jerky effort was just an approximation, a further adjustment brought the hand to its target and the rattle soon found its place in her mouth. I gently removed the rattle and placed it under the blanket lying in front of her. Rather than merely reaching under the blanket after her treasure she acted as though it no longer existed and her interest shifted to some nearby blocks.

COGNITIVE DEVELOPMENT

This infant had just demonstrated a lack of what Jean Piaget, the famous Swiss psychologist, called "object permanence" (Piaget and Inhelder, 1969). Piaget observed that very young children behave as though an object exists only as long as they can see it. Within a few months this little girl will acquire the basic concept of object permanence. [1]

As this child develops from an infant to a toddler she will not only begin to walk and run but she will begin the formidable task of learning her native language. However, significant as language acquisition may be, it is not the only intellectual step she must take.

She must acquire what Piaget has called the concept of "conservation." The pre-school child knows that objects do not cease to exist when they are out of sight but she may still believe that their number or volume changes with their shape--thus she may think there are more pennies when they are spread out than when they are grouped together, more dough when it is a long strip rather than a ball, or more water when it is poured from a wide glass into a taller one.

Later, having acquired the concepts of object permanence and conservation, our child has one

---

[1]. Even at this rudimentary level David Elkind (1970) sees the potential roots of a life-long religious quest for permanence and conservation. The object of concern will later be life itself and the answer to its apparent transitoriness may be found in the concept of God.

more major cognitive hurdle. Before adolescence children still think in very concrete terms. As they move out of childhood they gradually acquire the adult ability to think abstractly. This is the ability to conceive of possibilities beyond the present, to think of alternatives to the way things are, to consider all the possibilities and the consequences of each course of action. Having passed into adulthood she now has all of the basic abilities necessary to understand her world.

These brief examples of cognitive development illustrate one method of studying the process of growth and maturation which is the subject of "Developmental Psychology." The method illustrated may be called an "analysis by stages."[1] This same approach has been taken by other theorists to study different characteristics. So while Piaget discusses cognitive stages, Kohlberg discusses moral stages, Freud psycho-sexual stages, and Erikson psycho-social stages of development.

After a brief review of these major contributions to developmental psychology we will consider the question of whether or not the study of psychological development can aid in our understanding of religious development. Although religious development may quite naturally be included within the study of developmental psychology, more often it is relegated to the "psychology of religion." Thus we will be drawing upon two important sub-areas of psychology in this chapter, "Developmental Psychology" and the "Psychology of Religion."[2]

MORAL DEVELOPMENT

Although the main body of his work has dealt with the way an individual comes to know the world scientifically and mathematically, Piaget

---

[1] The examples given are not intended to be definitive. The stages defined by Piaget are somewhat more complex than these simple examples indicate.

[2] The psychology of religion is the study of psychological processes involved in religious behavior and experience. For a helpful introduction see Paloutzian, 1983.

([1932] 1965) has also studied the developing ability of the individual to understand the social world in moral terms. To do this he asked children to decide which of two boys should receive the more severe punishment--one who did a lot of damage accidentally, or one who deliberately disobeyed but did comparatively little physical damage.

A. A little boy who is called John is in his room. He is called to dinner. He goes into the dining room. But behind the door there was a chair, and on the chair was a tray with 15 cups on it. John couldn't have known that there was all this behind the door. He goes in; the door knocks against the tray; bang go the 15 cups, and they all get broken.

B. Once there was a little boy whose name was Henry. One day when his mother was out he tried to get some jam out of the cupboard. He climbed onto a chair and stretched out his arm. But the jam was too high up, and he couldn't reach it and have any. While he was trying to get it, he knocked over a cup. The cup fell down and broke.

Younger children say the first was worse, older children say the second--reflecting a change in their moral reasoning. This change, Piaget felt, was only possible as older children acquired the greater mental ability necessary to make moral judgments based on intentions rather than on the simple visible consequences of an act. Thus moral development is dependent upon cognitive development.

Lawrence Kohlberg (1969, 1973) has extended Piaget's work to include moral development at all ages. Although moral development is not as orderly as the development of some other characteristics, Kohlberg has identified six stages of development which he has grouped into three levels. (We will consider the three major levels without distinguishing the two separate stages possible at each level.) Like Piaget, Kohlberg studied moral development by analyzing the responses people give to a story which presents a moral dilemma.

88

One such story is the following, known as the "Heinz dilemna":

In Europe, a woman was near death from a special kind of cancer. There was one drug that doctors thought might save her. It was a form of radium that a druggist in the same town had recently discovered. The drug was expensive to make, but the druggist was charging ten times what the drug cost him to make. He paid $200 for the radium and charged $2,000 for a small dose of the drug. The sick woman's husband, Heinz, went to everyone he knew to borrow money, but he could only get together about $1,000, which is half of what it cost. He told the druggist that his wife was dying, and asked him to sell it cheaper or let him pay later. But the druggist said, "No, I discovered the drug and I'm going to make money from it." So Heinz got desperate and broke into the man's store to steal the drug for his wife.

Should Heinz have done that? Was it actually wrong or right? Why?

Because he was more interested in the structure than the content of thought, Kohlberg's analysis focussed more on the explanation or justification which was given than in the decision to steal or not to steal.

In the pre-adolescent and sometimes the adolescent or even adult, moral behavior is heavily dependent upon sets of rules; one obeys in order to avoid punishment. Reciprocity is an important principal at this stage: "An eye for an eye"; "You scratch my back and I'll scratch yours"; there is little thought of doing good for its own sake, or even for the good of society. The value of a human life is seen as instrumental to the satisfaction of the needs of its possessor or of other persons. Thus Heinz may have been justified because he loved his wife and he needed her--if he didn't love her he wouldn't be justified. This is what Kohlberg calls the "premoral" level.

With the development of the ability for abstract thought the adolescent acquires the capacity to take another person's point of view; to see that other

89

person seeing him; and to see a third person observing both. ("I see you seeing me; I compose the me I think you see"; and even, "I see you seeing me; I see you seeing me seeing you"--which begins to sound a bit like Dr. Seuss). This ability to take another's perspective leads to moral decision making on the basis of others' expectations--actions are right if they conform to the expectations of one's "significant others." Or if they involve doing what is generally expected of a person in his or her role (what a son **should** do, or a mother **should** do). Thus social and interpersonal factors become very important. (Heinz may have been justified because his wife was suffering and her family loved her.) This is the second level, the "morality of conventional role-conformity."

The third level of morality is what Kohlberg calls the "morality of self-accepted principles." At this level the individual formulates abstract ethical principles and conforms to them in order to avoid self-condemnation rather than punishment or public censure. This level is illustrated in the following response:

> By the law of society he was wrong but by the law of nature or of God the druggist was wrong and the husband was justified. Human life is above financial gain. Regardless of who was dying, if it was a total stranger, man has a duty to save him from dying. (Kohlberg, 1969, 244)

Kohlberg stresses the interaction of moral development with cognitive development and thus recognizes the importance of Piaget's pioneering work. However, Kohlberg's own work goes beyond the study of childhood, for he recognizes that while cognitive development is necessary for moral development, it is not sufficient in itself. Thus moral development may proceed in parallel with cognitive development or it may continue far into adulthood, long after the major steps in cognitive development have been taken.

PSYCHO-SEXUAL STAGES

Although the work of Piaget and Kohlberg has been relatively well accepted in contemporary psychology, the theories of Freud have proven

90

more controversial. Freud (1938) believed that the developing child progressed through three stages in each of which sexual pleasure was focussed on a specific area of the body. From birth to toilet training was the "oral" phase; during toilet training the "anal" phase; and roughly age three to five the "phallic" phase. With the resolution of the "Oedipus" (for boys) or "Electra" (for girls) complex (attraction to the opposite-sex parent; fear of the same-sex parent) at the end of the phallic phase, the groundwork of the personality is laid for life. This includes the individual's ideas of right and wrong, his or her ideals, and characteristic ways of reacting to frustration. Subsequent development proceeds through a (sexual) latency phase, and then a genital phase from puberty on into adulthood. However, the basic personality is established in childhood--"The child is father to the man." Freud's most important influence in developmental psychology has been his emphasis on the importance of events very early in an individual's life, and his stress on the influence of physical (Freud would say sexual) factors on psychological processes, often at an unconscious level.[1]

PSYCHO-SOCIAL STAGES

Erik Erikson has expanded and developed Freud's theories in a different direction. While not denying the importance of the "psycho-sexual" stages discussed by Freud, Erikson (1963) has emphasized social factors influencing the individual in "psycho-social" stages from birth to death. He has developed a description of eight stages of psychosocial development through which the individual moves from infancy to old age. In each of these stages there is a particular task or crisis which must be resolved. As each crisis is resolved in a positive way, there is a particular characteristic or virtue which emerges in the personality. If the crisis is resolved in a negative way a corresponding negative characteristic will dominate.

For example, in the first couple of years of life

---

[1] For a more detailed analysis see any textbook on Introductory Psychology or Personality Theory.

the task is one of learning "basic trust" versus "basic mistrust." During this stage the child is dependent upon adults, primarily the mother. The quality of care which the child receives will determine the degree to which the child is able to acquire a sense of trust in other people and in the world in general. However, there must always be some mistrust, or gullibility will result: it is the ratio between trust and mistrust which is important. If the mother's care is not only adequate, but consistent and reliable the child will develop feelings of security and basic trust. If the mother's care is inadequate, mistrust will dominate.[1]

This kind of psychological crisis or task takes place throughout each of the eight stages of psychosocial development. Underlying each of these crises is the individual's gradually developing sense of identity--from the infant's growing awareness of himself or herself as a separate being (who can control their own hand, but not the smiling face that hovers over them from time to time), to the individual at the end of life who has accepted the uniqueness yet inevitability of the life they have lived. Erikson (1963) identifies the eight stages and their antithetical outcomes as follows:

Oral-Sensory	0-1 yr	Trust/Mistrust
Muscular-Anal	1-3 yrs	Autonomy/Shame, Doubt
Locomotor-Genital	3-5	Initiative/Guilt
Latency	6-11 yrs	Industry/Inferiority
Adolescence	12-18 yrs	Indentity/Role Confusion
Young Adulthood	19-35 yrs	Intimacy/Isolation
Adulthood	35-50 yrs	Generativity/Stagnation
Maturity	50+ yrs	Ego Integrity/Despair

The ages given for each stage are approximations. There is considerable variation in ages between individuals in the last three stages.

---

[1]. The psychological strength or virtue gained at this stage is hope. Trust becomes the basis for hope, according to Erikson, and hope is the foundation of the adult's faith in some form of institutionalized religion.

In summary, each of these theorists, Piaget, Kohlberg, Freud, Erikson, has emphasized one characteristic of the individual and shown how it develops through a series of steps or stages. Within their own particular emphasis they share the following assumptions:

1. The stages are **sequential**. That is, they come one after another in a logically necessary fashion.

2. The sequence is **invariant**. Stages cannot be skipped or missed out.

3. The sequence of stages is **universal**. The rate of progression through the stages, which may vary slightly within a culture, may vary somewhat more between different cultures, but the same stages in the same sequence would be found in all cultures.

While making these basic assumptions, each theorist nevertheless recognizes that an individual at one stage may continue to show characteristics of an earlier stage of development. Furthermore, for Piaget and Kohlberg, at least, attainment of the highest level is by no means universal.

With the exception of Erikson, and to a lesser extent Kohlberg, these theorists have largely ignored adult development in their emphasis on the importance of early childhood and adolescence. More recently however, developmental psychology as well as popular interest has focussed increasing attention on adulthood, and significant stages have been identified in the lives of adults at mid-life. [1]

As we have noted, parenthetically, some psychologists have attempted to explain certain religious experiences on the basis of developing psychological functions. This possibility raises certain questions in many Christians' minds, and it is to this issue which we now turn our attention.

---

[1]. Some of these developments are documented in the works of Levinson, 1978; Sheehy, 1976; Eichorn, Clausen, Hann, Honzik, and Musaen, 1981; and Hepworth and Featherstone, 1982.

CONTROVERSIAL ISSUE

Developmental psychology has made significant strides in its attempt to understand the growth and development of the individual from birth to death. It has identified critical periods for a variety of important themes in the life-cycle. However, one very important theme has received only scant attention. This theme is the individual's evolving concern for religious issues. The question then arises,

---

Can developmental psychology aid in the understanding of religious development?

In using the term "religious" we mean something along the line of William James' definition: "the feelings, acts, and experiences of individual men in their solitude, so far as they apprehend themselves to stand in relation to whatever they may consider the divine" ([1902] 1960, 50). Although we will further restrict this definition to the Christian religion, and may substitute the word "spiritual," we are not concerned, primarily, with church organizations or their doctrines, but with the individual's own religious/spiritual experience and understanding of his relationship to God. What then does psychology have to do with this experience and understanding?

PSYCHOLOGY IS IRRELEVANT

In considering this question we see once again psychology and Christianity standing "toe to toe." Because of psychology's inability to distinguish the secular from the sacred, Christians often fear the scientific study of their experience will profane and destroy it. "Religious experience is not a psychological event; it is a mystical spiritual relationship," they say. "Religious awareness is a gift from God; it is not a predictable laboratory phenomenon" ("the wind blows where it wishes...so is every one who is born of the Spirit," Jhn 3:8).

94

Christians see the experiences of conviction, repentance, faith, sanctification, as spiritual only. Where there may be obvious psychological parallels these are seen as mere consequences of a primarily spiritual phenomenon. Many Christians are aware of past skirmishes with psychology which resulted in the declaration, that a treasured religious experience was "nothing but..." (e.g., wish fulfillment, or sublimation, or an unconscious projection, etc.) and they are skeptical of any psychological perspective on religion. As William James points out:

> Such cold-blooded assimilations threaten, we think, to undo our soul's vital secrets, as if the same breath which should succeed in explaining their origin would simultaneously explain away their significance, and make them appear of no more preciousness, either, than the useful groceries of which M. Taine speaks. ([1902] 1960, 32)

With this in mind many Christians would answer our question, "Can psychology aid in the understanding of religious development?" with a resounding "No!"

PSYCHOLOGY IS RELEVANT

In taking the positive perspective on this issue, the first thing we must point out is the false dichotomy assumed by the "nothing but" statement above. As we discussed in Chapter 1, an explanation on one level does not invalidate explanations on one or more other levels. Specifically, this means that just because a physiologist explains an action in terms of nerve impulses, glandular secretions, and muscle contractions, it does not mean that a psychologist's explanation in terms of learning and motivation is unnecessary, nor does it mean that the theologian's explanation in the spiritual realm is invalid. Rather, each description can contribute something valuable to our total understanding (recall the analogy of the blind men and the elephant in Chapter 1). With this in mind the responsible psychologist studying religious phenomena is careful to acknowledge his limitations, as does Gordon Allport:

95

My effort, as I say, is directed solely to a portrayal of the place of subjective religion in the structure of the personality whenever and wherever religion has such a place. My approach is psychological, some would call it naturalistic. I make no assumptions and no denials regarding the claims of revealed religion. Writing as a scientist I am not entitled to do either. (1950, xi)

Psychology, even the psychology of religion, is the study of behavior and mental events, and does not judge the veracity of supernatural claims. The affirmative answer to our question, however, goes further and asks, "Does psychology have a **positive** contribution to make?"

One positive reason for studying individual development, both physical and psychological, is to better understand the common biblical metaphor of growth.[1] The value of studying the growth process is thus seen in the wider (even spiritual) applicability of some general conclusions of contemporary psychological study. For example:

1. Experiences early in the developmental cycle have far-reaching effects.

2. Growth often proceeds in fairly discrete stages.

3. Early stages must be mastered before later ones. ("You must walk before you run.")

Each of these observations may be applied to growth in the spiritual realm as well. In this way a thorough understanding of the processes of physical and psychological growth may in turn contribute to a better understanding of the biblical metaphor.

However, the greatest value for Christians of an understanding of developmental psychology is in

---

[1]. "When I was a child, I used to speak as a child, think as a child, reason as a child; when I became a man, I did away with childish things" (I Cor. 13:11); "We are no longer to be children...but speaking the truth in love, we are to grow up in all aspects into Him, who is the head, even Christ" (Eph. 4:14).

recognizing the ways in which spiritual and psychological processes may affect each other directly.

Psychological/spiritual interdependence. One evening on a camping trip several years ago, my wife and I listened outside the tent as our five-year-old Joelle and three-year-old Matthew tried to get to sleep. Always the "mother," Joelle attempted to dispel her little brother's fear of bears and other wild creatures by reminding him that Jesus was watching over them. Not content with generalities, he responded "Does Jesus got a gun?"

Here we see some of the limitations of childhood religious experience. Most parents are familiar with not only the delightful simplicity of childhood faith but also the many (from an adult perspective) conceptual incongruities. And most Christians recognize the existence of these limitations. Some Christians speak of a particular "age of accountability" prior to which a child is presumed to be incapable of fully grasping the central concepts of the faith. In recognizing childhood limitations they are acknowledging the interdependence of psychological and religious development. However, much work remains to be done, both in basic research and in informing Christian parents, on this interdependence.[1]

One of the most critical times of development is adolescence. It is a time of upheaval physically, psychologically, socially, and often spiritually. It is also a time when it is extremely important to appreciate the interdependence of these various influences. Because of the importance of this period we will consider it in greater detail as an example of the way psychology can aid in the understanding of religious development.

Religion in adolescence. Confronted with questions from their young adolescent about the problem of evil in the world, or conflicts between

---

[1]. For some good theoretical beginnings see the work of Allport, 1950; Ballard & Fleck, 1985; Elkind, 1970; Fowler, 1981; Strommen, 1971; Wright, 1982. For practical Christian applications see Darling, 1969; Dobson, 1970; Wilson, 1982.

science and faith, parents are often caught off-guard and may accuse the school or church youth group. However, an appreciation of the cognitive, moral, and personality growth taking place at this time would help prepare them for this new growth. Each of these areas has an important influence on developing religious awareness.

For example, the new ability to deal with abstract intellectual and moral issues is a characteristic of Piaget's fourth stage of cognitive development. In testing out this new ability the adolescent may enjoy "intellectual sparring" over religious issues. Their developing ability to take another's perspective, and growing social awareness creates a need for a more personal God. Their concern with identity leads them to search for a God who understands the mysterious depths of the personality which are such a puzzle to them. (One of my teen-age daughter's favorite songs is titled "You know me better than I know myself.") These factors, together with their developing power for moral reasoning and their awareness of greater and greater moral problems, may be the trigger for dramatic changes in religious faith.

For example, children in the early to mid-elementary years judge morality in terms of reciprocity. Quite logically, they think of God in these terms too. In this stage they think that if we do good, God rewards us; if we do evil, God punishes us--often immediately. They order the universe in moral terms. God is like a stern but just parent (of course many adults still see God in this way). Now, usually in the pre-teen, but certainly by the early teen years, the individual is brought face to face with evil and suffering and asks, "How can a just God allow such suffering?"

Around the end of the Vietnam War Fowler (1983) reports interviewing an eleven-year-old girl. When asked about God, she said, "Don't believe in God...God is asleep." She then talked about seeing a picture of a little Vietnamese girl with napalm sticking to her body in burning globs, running down the street. The eleven-year-old said, "Any God who can let that happen has to be asleep. So don't believe in God." (Fowler calls the many young people like her "11-year-old atheists.") Fowler says what had died there was not God, but her image of God, one structured along the lines of strict moral reciprocity.

Between eleven and thirteen is a time when young people, often not so dramatically, but with the same sort of seriousness, have to relinquish one way of constructing the universe, one way of making sense of it, and construct a new one. This new stage, or way of seeing the universe, will be broader and more flexible. The young girl in our example may construct her image of God in terms of personality and feeling. By fourteen, she may emerge with a view of God that takes more account of the presence of evil in the world, human freedom, and the misuse of freedom. She might see God again as a caring Being, who in some sense is working to overcome and redeem the pain in the world.

The transition to this stage is very important and frequently difficult. However, in a Christian community, the local church, it is usually successful (there are other perils ahead). The influence of parents, the local church, Christian friends, and Christian authors who provide answers to some of the perplexing problems are all helpful. The young teen is looking for a broader and more inclusive faith, but is not usually questioning the whole basis of faith--that often comes later. At this point they are ready to accept the faith of "significant others" (heroes, peers, and even teachers and parents). So while it is a shift, an expansion in beliefs, it is not usually a rejection of belief.

However, just as any time the boat is rocked there is danger, so parents should be aware of the need for new answers, and a broader perspective. This is difficult if parents have never dealt with the problems themselves, but other Christians, writers, and teachers have, and may be helpful.

However, all is not settled. The young people with whom I deal, people in their late teens and early twenties, frequently pass through another time of significant struggle. I have seen many young people reared in Christian families, and conservative evangelical churches, apparently reject Christianity during this time. After the transition into adolescence, and a period of

99

apparent stability in their faith, frequently marked by "conversion," "baptism," or "re-dedication" experiences, suddenly there is an eruption of doubt and questioning. This is not in itself unbelief--an important point to keep in mind. The individual wants to believe but many of the "pat" answers accepted earlier are now re-examined and sometimes found wanting.

Here, perhaps more than at any other period, it is important to recognize underlying psychological processes. The primary psychological task of adolescents is the development of an identity--their view of themselves which integrates their varied past experiences and projects an acceptable future. In a Christian context, religious beliefs are a critical component of this overall identity (Philipchalk and Sifft, 1985). However, a truly "achieved" identity is one which has been freely chosen after having considered various other options. Consequently a time of examination and questioning is inevitable. Although this may be diffused over a longer period, for some it is a brief time of intense struggle. The eventual result is usually exhaustion and a realization of the ultimate necessity of faith. However, the new beliefs, which may very well be the old ones, are now truly the individual's own.

Parents, pastors, and counselors, who quite naturally are concerned at this stage, need to be aware that while there is indeed a spiritual dimension to the struggle (although it may be more related to doctrinal issues than to faith) there are also important psychological issues involved. In my experience, the most helpful thing a person can do at this time is to listen, accept and love the individual, allowing time and opportunity to express doubts, but avoiding condemnation or pressure to make significant (e.g., career or marriage) decisions.

Other ages. Religious development may be significantly affected by psychological development both in the young child and in the adolescent. Recently several authors have also identified psychological factors in adulthood which may affect religious growth, especially in mid-life and again in old age.[1] The famous analyst Carl Jung is said to have observed that he never treated a person older than 39 whose problem was not basically a spiritual one. Thus the psychological and the spiritual continue to interact throughout life.

To summarize, we have seen that fear of psychological study of religious development is unfounded, being based on the false assumption that a psychological approach would "explain away" precious religious experience. We have also noted that there may be value in a better understanding of physical and psychological growth for the simple reason that in scripture spiritual growth is frequently likened to physical growth. Finally, we noted some important instances of the direct influence of psychological processes on religious concerns, leading to the conclusion that the study of developmental psychology may be of great benefit to the better understanding of religious development.

DISCUSSION QUESTIONS

Age of accountability. We made reference to the "age of accountability" as the time at which a child is able to grasp, in a meaningful way, the essentials of a religious faith. Assuming there is a theological basis for this concept, what is the psychological evidence? What are the separate and interacting influences of cognitive, emotional, moral, and social development?

Moral development in women. The work of Lawrence Kohlberg on moral development is well recognized. However, it must be noted that his conclusions apply largely to males. What of moral development in women? It would be unwise to assume it is the same as in men. Does moral development proceed differently in males and females? Do men and women make moral and ethical decisions differently?[2]

Guilt. One of the most significant developments

---

[1]. See Conway, 1980; White and White, 1980.
[2]   For additional information see the work by Carol Gilligan (1977, 1984, 1985).

in childhood, from both a secular and Christian point of view, is a conscience with its attendant guilt. Is guilt simply a conditioned emotional response (as the behaviorist might say)? Is it the result of conflict with the superego (as a psychoanalyst would say)? Is it the failure to live up to our self-concept (as the humanist might say)? Is it the voice of the Holy Spirit? Or is it some combination of these?[1]

Death. Secular psychologists see death as final. As Christians we see resurrection beyond, with death being but another step in that direction. What implications do our beliefs have for the process of dying?

As medical technology has advanced death has become more and more difficult to define. We need to focus our attention less on preserving the physical and more on preserving the "personhood" of the individual (cf. Evans, 1970). This means giving greater attention to our concept of the dying person created in the image of God (as the abortion issue has forced us to do at the other end of life). When is personhood sacrificed to technical efficiency? Should we advocate a more "natural death?" What is "natural death?" How far does one go in "allowing" natural death?

Genetics. A host of issues from the burgeoning study of genetics are relevant here. As Christians we must ask, "What are the implications for the child, the parent(s), and society, of artificial insemination, "test-tube" babies, surrogate mothers, and genetic engineering?" The Catholic Church is taking a position on these issues: Protestant Christians need to give them careful thought too.[2]

---

[1] For help on this issue and an important distinction between false and true guilt see Counts and Narramore, 1970; Narramore, 1984; Tournier, 1962.

[2] For an interesting presentation of some new problems associated with medical advances see Andrews (1984). For a helpful discussion of some moral and religious aspects of genetic engineering see Ellison (1977). Some of these issues as well as a provocative discussion of abortion are contained in Smith (1985).

Doubt. The subject of doubt was mentioned briefly above. Conyers (1984) argues that doubt may serve a very useful function but that unfortunately Christians have misunderstood it. When is doubt valuable? What is its role in religious development? How is it to be distinguished from unbelief?

Psychology of religion. The psychology of religion was introduced in this chapter as being relevant to the study of religious development. This field raises many other issues of interest to Christians. For example, what is the role of psychological processes in conversion, healing (see Chapter 2), mystical experiences, and glossolalia (see Chapter 4)?

In conclusion, our examination of developmental psychology has focussed on the issue of its relevance for religious development. This approach has largely ignored the obvious contribution of developmental psychology to the general task of child-rearing. Nevertheless, we have seen that the areas of developmental psychology and the psychology of religion have important contributions to make to a Christian understanding of human growth. As thoughtful Christians continue to deal with controversial issues in these two fields they further the ongoing task of relating psychology and Christianity.

SUGGESTED READINGS

Allport, G. 1950. The individual and his religion. New York: MacMillan. A classic which deals not only with the role of religion in development, especially adolescence, but also with the role of religion in the healthy adult personality.

Cully, I. V. 1979. Christian child development. New York: Harper & Row. Discusses the religious development of children using the theories of Erikson, Piaget, Skinner, Kohlberg, and others. Uses examples and biblical references.

Fowler, J. 1983, November. Stages of faith. Psychology Today, pp.56-62. Interview and brief overview of Fowler's rather complex but important theory (based on Piaget, Erikson, and Kohlberg) as developed in his book (1981).

Narramore, B. 1984. No condemnation. Grand Rapids, MI: Zondervan. Thorough and very helpful discussion of the proper role of guiltin human experience as well as a very clear elucidation of the way it is widely misunderstood and misused.

REFERENCES AND OTHER SOURCES

Allport, G. 1950. The individual and his religion. New York: MacMillan.

Andrews, L.B. 1984, December. Yours, mine and theirs. Psychology Today, 18, 20-29.

Ballard, S., & Fleck, J. 1975. The teaching of religious concepts: A three stage model. Journal of Psychology and Theology, 3, 164-171.

Conway, S. 1980. You and your husband's mid-life crisis. Elgin, IL: David C. Cook.

Conyers, A. 1984, February. When doubt can help you. Christianity Today, pp. 34-35.

Counts, W., & Narramore, B. 1974. Freedom from guilt. Santa Ana: Harvest House.

Cully, I.V. 1979. Christian child development. New York: Harper & Row.

Darling, H. 1969. Man in triumph. Grand Rapids, MI: Zondervan.

Dobson, J. 1970. Dare to discipline. Wheaton, IL: Tyndale.

Eichorn, D., Clausen, J., Hann, N., Honzik, M., and Musaen, P. 1981. Present and past in middle life. San Francisco: Academic Press.

Elkind, D. 1970. The origins of religion in the child. Review of Religious Research, 12, 35-42.

Ellison, C.W., ed. 1977. Modifying man: Implications and ethics. Washington, DC: University Press of America.

Erikson, E. 1963. Childhood and society (2nd ed.). New York: Norton.

Evans, C. 1977 Preserving the person: A look at the human sciences. Downers Grove, IL: InterVarsity Press.

104

Fowler, J. 1981. Stages of Faith: The psychology of human development and the quest for meaning. San Francisco: Harper and Row.

Fowler, J. 1983, November. Stages of faith. Psychology Today, pp.56-62.

Freud, S. 1938. Three contributions to the theory of sex. In Brill, A.A., ed. The basic writings of Sigmund Freud. New York: Random House.

Hepworth, M. & Featherstone, M. 1982. Surviving male middle age. Oxford: Basil Blackwell.

James, W. [1902] 1960. Varieties of religious experience. London: Fontana.

Kohlberg, L. 1969. Stage and sequence: The cognitive-developmental approach to socialization. In Goslin, D.A., ed. Handbook of socialization theory and research. Chicago: Rand McNally.

Kohlberg, L. 1973. Implications of developmental psychology for education: Examples from moral development. Educational Psychologist, 10, 2-14.

Levinson, D.J. 1978. The seasons of a man's life. New York: Alfred A. Knopf.

Narramore, B. 1984. No condemnation. Grand Rapids, MI: Zondervan.

Paloutzian, R. 1983. Invitation to the psychology of religion. Glenview, IL: Scott, Foresman.

Philipchalk, R., & Sifft, C. 1985. Role of religious commitment in occupational and overall identity formation in college students. Journal of Psychology and Christianity.4(1), 44-47.

Piaget, J. [1932] 1965. The moral judgement of the child. New York: Free Press.

Piaget, J., & Inhelder, B. 1969. The psychology of the child. (H. Weaver, Trans.). New York: Basic Books.

Sheehy, G. 1976. Passages. predictable crises of adult life. New York: Bantam Books.

Smith, H. 1985, January. A legacy of life. Christianity Today, 29(1), 18-25.

Strommen, M. 1971. Research on religious development: A comprehensive handbook. New York: Hawthorne Books.

Tournier, P. 1962. Guilt and grace. New York: Harper and Row.

White, J., & White, M. 1980. The Christian in mid-life. Colorado Springs: NavPress.

Wilson, E. 1982. You try being a teenager. Portland, OR: Multnomah Press.

Wright, J., Jr. 1982. Erikson: Identity and religion. New York: Seabury.

CHAPTER 6: LEARNING AND COGNITION

OPERANT CONDITIONING
CLASSICAL CONDITIONING
CONTROVERSIAL ISSUE

Should Christians use conditioning techniques?

Response
COGNITIVE BEHAVIORAL PSYCHOLOGY
AN EXAMPLE
Antecedents and consequents
Rewards
Shaping
The cognitive component
Other behaviors
HABITS: A VALUABLE ALLY
DISCUSSION QUESTIONS
Free will
Reward versus punishment
Language
Artificial intelligence
SUGGESTED READINGS
REFERENCES AND OTHER SOURCES

107

There was a slow stirring of the water moving steadily around the pool. Suddenly it stopped. For a few seconds the surface of the pool was calm as the audience held its breath. And then like an explosion from the deep eight tons of killer whale burst out of the water and with a graceful twist gently nudged the ball high in the air before falling back into the water with a resounding crash.

In another pool sea lions were catching rings, balancing balls, and performing numerous other tricks to the immense delight of their audience.

How was all this accomplished? Were these animals of extraordinary, almost human intelligence? Did their trainers have some special insight into the "animal psyche"?

As any student of psychology knows a great deal of research effort has gone into the study of learning in animals, usually pigeons and white rats. The well known psychologist B.F. Skinner and his students have trained pigeons to play ping-pong, to act as quality-control inspectors, and even to guide missiles to their target. The whales, the sea lions, the pigeons and the rats were all trained through a procedure psychologists call "operant conditioning."

OPERANT CONDITIONING

Operant conditioning is the name given to the process of strengthening a response, that is, making a response more likely, by giving the animal something it wants (a reward or reinforcer) whenever the response occurs. Difficult behaviors can be taught by giving a reward for closer and closer approximations to the ultimately desired response. This is called "shaping" of the response. Thus, when you are teaching Fido to roll over you may give him a biscuit in the beginning when he lies down, later when he lies down and rolls onto his side, and eventually only when he lies down and rolls over completely. You have shaped his behavior using operant conditioning. Individual behaviors acquired in this way may also be joined together, or "chained", to form even more complex behaviors.

Reinforcers exert a powerful control over behavior in both animals and man. Governments give medals and prestige to their outstanding citizens, employers pay salaries and bonuses to get the job done, teachers give good grades, advancement, and time off to successful students, and parents give allowances, rewards, and praise, when children complete various duties.

Behavior may change dramatically when reinforcements which are already present in the situation are simply made dependent ("contingent") upon the desired behavior, as when the attention which Johnny gets for disrupting the class is no longer given for the disruptive behavior but rather for sitting quietly and doing his work; or an allowance which had been automatic is made contingent upon having certain chores done.

More elaborate applications of these principles have been made through what are called "token economies." In a token economy, desirable behaviors are rewarded with tokens which can be redeemed for more substantial rewards later. Each desired behavior has a clearly defined value in tokens. Dramatic results are often obtained as desirable behaviors are rapidly substituted for undesirable. Token economies have been used in mental hospitals, as well as in classroom settings with delinquent children, "normal" children, and the mentally retarded (Atthowe and Krasner, 1968; Kazdin and Bootzin, 1972; O'Leary and Drabman, 1971).

You may have noticed that our discussion has jumped without a break from the training of whales and rats to the training of humans. According to Skinner both human and animal behavior is controlled by its consequences. Skinner makes no distinction between animals and humans in this regard.

There can be no doubt that Skinner has identified a powerful influence over behavior. But is he justified in his extrapolations from animal studies to human behavior? Even if we include less obvious rewards, such as approval, or the flexibility of intermittent schedules of reinforcement, is this approach sufficient to explain virtually **all** behavior (the only exception being that dealt with below)?

CLASSICAL CONDITIONING

Similar questions have been raised concerning the other major type of learning identified by researchers. In 1901 the Russian physiologist Ivan Pavlov noticed that if a stimulus such as a bell was consistently presented before food was given to the dogs he was studying, the saliva would begin to flow in the dogs' mouths when the bell was rung. The salivation response was said to have been conditioned to the bell. This procedure, which came to be known as classical or respondant conditioning, is different from the instrumental or operant conditioning studied by Skinner primarily in that with classical conditioning the unconditioned response (UCR) (e.g., salivation) being reflexive, is elicited or "drawn out" of the animal through the presentation of the unconditioned stimulus (UCS) (e.g., food in the mouth), whereas in operant conditioning the response is emitted or "volunteered" by the animal.

Although classical conditioning may seem to be a more basic and therefore less useful type of learning for humans, several instructive applications have been made. One of the best known experiments in psychology involved the classical conditioning of fear in an infant known as "Little Albert." Initially Little Albert was given a variety of objects to play with, including a white rat. One day while he was happily playing with the rat the experimenters sounded a terrifying noise behind him. After doing this several times Little Albert became afraid of the rat and would cry if it was brought near him.[1]

Speculating that many fears may be learned this way, including the intense irrational fears called "phobias," psychologists have developed a technique for eliminating these fears based on laboratory experiments with classical conditioning. The procedure, known as "extinction," involves the

---

[1]. This experiment, conducted in 1920, would not be permitted today under the code of ethics of the American Psychological Association.

weakening of the (conditioned) fear response through presentation of the (conditioned) fear producing object (e.g., the white rat), without the (unconditioned) fear producing stimulus (e.g., the terrifying noise). When extinction is approached more gradually, perhaps by imagining objects or situations which are increasingly similar to the feared object or situation, before imagining the feared object or situation, the process is called "systematic desensitization." Usually a new response, relaxation, which is incompatible with the fear response, is deliberately associated with the feared object or situation. The result is a substitution of relaxation for fear through a process called "reciprocal inhibition."[1]

These procedures, while they may be effective in eliminating specific fears, have been criticized for ignoring a presumed underlying problem and merely dealing with the symptoms. If the underlying problem is not dealt with, the elimination of one symptom will only result in another symptom being substituted for it.

CONTROVERSIAL ISSUE

Many people, both Christian and non-Christian, object to the application to human behavior of principles of learning which are based upon studies of animals in a laboratory. Some, such as Jay Adams (1973) criticize efforts like James Dobson's (1970) to apply what they see as a "Godless behaviorism" to human beings. They say that man is much more than an animal--to assume otherwise is degrading. And they feel that treating humans as animals is manipulative and results only in superficial change at best.

Thus we pose the question:

> ## Should Christians use conditioning techniques?

---

[1] For a helpful discussion of these and related techniques from a Christian perspective see Koteskey, 1983, p. 156 ff.

Response. In response to this question I would like to outline three arguments for a proper appreciation of the importance of principles of conditioning in human behavior. I should point out however, that acceptance of the importance of conditioning does not imply acceptance of Skinner's complete philosophical position. This position, as outlined in his popular book Beyond Freedom and Dignity is sometimes called "radical behaviorism." Starting with the basic assumption that all behavior is completely determined or controlled by environmental conditions, Skinner logically and honestly draws the conclusion that the concepts of freedom and dignity are then unnecessary illusions. As Cosgrove (1982), and Schaeffer (1972), have pointed out, such a position is clearly contrary to a biblical view of man. Consequently, the church has historically had a bias against behavioral techniques because of the philosophy with which they have been associated. We must indeed be cautious in accepting procedures based on unacceptable assumptions. Furthermore, we must not be guilty of a simplistic "if it works, do it" rationale.

Nevertheless, in spite of these objections, we must be careful not to "throw out the baby with the bath water." Before denying any implications of animal studies we should consider the following points:

1. Humans are similar to animals in many ways.

2. So-called "higher processes" such as thoughts and attitudes often **follow** changes in behavior which may often be brought about by simple procedures.

3. Although at times we may be "creatures of habit," we have the power to control our habits.

First, it should not surprise us to find that in many ways humans are like animals. It is because of the similarity in their physical bodies that drugs and surgical procedures can be tried on animals before humans. The Bible often refers to man as a creature or beast (e.g., Ps. 49; Eccles. 3:18-21). Certainly he is different from animals in many ways and has certain "God-like" characteristics as

112

discussed by Koteskey (1980); but he does have many "animal-like" characteristics as Koteskey has also pointed out.

> ...techniques of shaping behavior, developed in the animal laboratory, work well applied to humans with some specific types of subject matter....some of these things do work because humans are similar to animals with regard to their finiteness....we must recognize the creatureliness of humans. Like the rest of creation, they are dependent upon the Creator for everything. (Koteskey, 1980, 19)

We must be careful not to think more highly of ourselves than we ought. Conditioning techniques may be very helpful in understanding and controlling certain aspects of our "creatureliness."

In a more recent work for Christian counselors Koteskey (1983) gives the example of his eighteen month old son who developed an intense fear of dogs after two unpleasant experiences with them. Even the fact that the child was too young to talk did not prevent a fellow Christian psychologist from concluding that he had a spiritual problem. We should recognize that not every problem is necessarily a spiritual one. Just as a disturbance may have a purely biological cause, so too it may have a simple psychological (learning) explanation. Information gained from the study of animals may be helpful in the understanding of psychological problems as it is often vital in understanding biological problems.

A second consideration is that the relationship between thinking and behaving is not always as it may seem. One of the reasons we may disparage attempts to change behavior through the simple manipulation of rewards and punishments is that we see such change as superficial and temporary. We assume that true and lasting change comes only through attitude change; we behave as we think, and not vice versa. However, research in this area suggests this is not always the case. For example, if subjects in an experiment are induced to perform an action contrary to their beliefs, they often change their beliefs to be consistent with their new

113

behavior (Festinger, 1964). After reviewing numerous experiments with similar findings, Meyers (1983) concludes:

> It is true that we sometimes stand up for what we believe, but it is also true that we will believe in what we stand up for. If social psychology has taught us anything during the last twenty-five years, it is that **we are likely not only to think ourselves into a way of acting but also to act ourselves into a way of thinking.** (44)

As the 19th century Christian writer Juliana H. Ewing (1841-1885) notes, "If one fights for good behavior, God makes one a present of the good feelings." Thus, the control of external responses may be neither as superficial nor as temporary as we sometimes assume.

A third important point we must keep in mind is that while we may be somewhat animal-like in the ways we acquire habits, and while we may be influenced by our habits much more than we know, we nevertheless can become aware of our habits and use them for our good.

As we learn a new response and repeat it over and over, it gradually becomes habitual. A habit may become so automatic that we are no longer aware of it much less the precise environmental conditions which triggered it. Nevertheless, if by conscious effort, or through the help of others we are made aware of a habit, we may purposely change the environmental conditions so that the habitual response is no longer triggered (the compulsive eater removes attractive food from the house); or, on the other hand, we may just as purposely train ourselves to a new habitual response to the old conditions (when hunger pangs strike we direct our friend's attention to celery sticks instead of potato chips). The point is that while habits may control a large amount of our behavior, we have the power to choose and change those habits by choosing and changing the controlling conditions (environmental or otherwise). This interaction of choice and environmental determinism has been called "reciprocal determinism" by the social-learning theorist Albert Bandura. Thus, to accept the importance of habits learned by the same principles in animals and people, is not necessarily to accept the assumption of complete environmental determinism for both animals and people. People have animal-like characteristics and may learn in ways very similar to animals. Nevertheless, they can become aware of these ways and consequently manipulate their own learning.

Most of us grossly underestimate the influence habits have on us. William James (1900) in his discourse on habits quotes the Duke of Wellington as saying, "Habits second nature? Habit is ten times nature." Each day we perform innumerable acts with very little conscious thought. The way we walk, dress, brush our teeth, eat our food, is so "automatic" that if the habitual pattern is interrupted, the whole behavior may become cumbersome and inefficient (try starting in a different place when you brush your teeth). Habits are useful; indeed they are necessary. Their very utility resides in the fact that they allow us to perform complex behaviors very frequently, over and over, "without thinking." They are the "automatic pilot" the "cruise control" of our behavioral repertoire.

However, it is this very lack of thought which constitutes a possible danger. Who of us has not been annoyed by another's habits? More importantly, a lack of appreciation for the power of habit ("...ten times nature") deprives us of a powerful ally in attaining goals for our behavior. Too often we attempt to change our behavior through sheer force of will-power, and the result is discouragement. We muster all of our determination and bring it to bear on a certain behavior. This may be a problem with overeating, smoking, or public speaking, or even a failure to have a regular time of personal devotions, or to think on spiritual things and be aware of the presence of God. But because our efforts are based solely on good intentions and will-power, without an appreciation of the strength of habits, or the principles by which they are acquired or eliminated, we quickly become discouraged, and old habits regain their ground.

Many Christians are not aware of the vast amount of research done by psychologists on the acquisition and elimination of habits. Even those who are aware of this work may not be aware of significant new insights which have potential for application to a wider variety of problems, including specifically Christian interests (e.g., Ratcliff, 1978).

In the next section we turn to a relatively recent development in the study of human learning, "cognitive behavioral psychology," and consider a practical application for Christians.

COGNITIVE BEHAVIORAL PSYCHOLOGY

Historically, the study of learning or habit acquisition has concentrated on animal behavior and largely non-verbal behavior in humans. More recently however, attention has shifted to the important role played by cognitive events (thoughts, beliefs, images) in human learning. The recognition and analysis of cognitive events is an important way in which the study of human learning has gone beyond animal research. One result has been the development of what is called "cognitive behavioral psychology."

A further move within this field has been the recognition that the principles of behavioral psychology may be applied to change one's **own** behavior. This practical development is known by such terms as "Self-Directed Behavior" (Watson and Tharpe, 1981) or "Self-Management" (Williams and Long, 1983). In this approach individuals are encouraged to monitor their own behavior and then to apply the principles of behavioral psychology themselves. This approach has been successfully applied to a wide variety of problems.[1] Moreover, it is a small step to substitute biblically inspired goals. I have worked with my students in applying these techniques successfully to change habits of

---

[1] For applications to smoking see Danaher and Lichtenstein, 1978, to drinking see Miller and Munoz, 1976, to weight loss see Stuart and Davis, 1972, to time management see Lakein, 1974, to studying see Robinson, 1970, to family problems see Paterson and Gullion, 1971, to assertiveness see Bower and Bower, 1978, and to depression see Beck and Greenberg, 1974.

overeating, sarcasm, nervous "tics," smoking, drinking alcohol, as well as strengthening habits of Bible reading, prayer, positive thinking, jogging, public speaking, studying, and others.

AN EXAMPLE

As an example let us consider the habit of a time of personal devotions (Bible study and prayer). This is probably one of the greatest sources of frustration today for Christians who desire to grow in their relationship with God. Most would admit the importance of this daily discipline, and yet an almost equal number would admit to spending little or no time in consistent personal Bible study and prayer. Therefore, the example of establishing a habit of morning devotions will be used as an illustration. This of course is only one of countless behaviors which we could modify; it is used as an example because of its simplicity and its potential value. In selecting a target behavior it is important that it be simple and easily identifiable.[1] This does not mean that we can deal with only simple (and insignificant) behaviors, but that more complex behaviors must be broken down into their simpler components and dealt with individually. Later they can be linked together to form the more complex "chains" from which they were derived.

Antecedents and consequents. The first principle in the modification of behavior is that behavior is seen as a function of "antecedent" and "consequent" conditions. That is, no matter how strong a disposition or habit may be the behavior will not occur unless the correct circumstances are present (antecedent conditions). Similarly, regardless of how correct or appropriate the circumstances may be the behavior will not be maintained if it does not produce desirable consequences. By manipulating these two, a powerful control over behavior is gained.

---

[1] The target behavior should be monitored and a careful record kept before, during, and after the behavior change program. Sometimes the mere act of keeping track of the behavior produces desirable change.

Those who would spend more time in Bible study must establish the right antecedents (time, place, Bible), for no matter how hard they desire their goal they will not attain it without these. They would also be wise to arrange positive consequences for performing the act, especially in the early stages of habit development. Although Bible study carries with it intrinsic rewards as the Holy Spirit illuminates the Scriptures to us, incompatible responses such as remaining in bed also contain rewards, and in addition are much more firmly established. During initial stages then, when intrinsic rewards are weak and old habits are strong, additional rewards should be arranged.

Rewards. Possible rewards include feelings of satisfaction and accomplishment which may be delivered cognitively through self-instructions (e.g., "There, I've completed another study. I've accomplished something worthwhile."). On the other hand, rewards may be more concrete. Any desirable situation which is made contingent upon a behavior will strengthen that behavior. Early morning devotions, for example, may be rewarded by a shower, or breakfast, providing one is willing to make these contingent upon the new behavior, foregoing them if the behavior is not performed. However, a more desirable approach is to institute new forms of reward so that the net result of the behavior change program is an increase in reward. While concrete rewards may be given each time the behavior is performed, a more practical approach is to keep a record of the behavior, giving tokens (e.g., a check mark in a book, or on the calendar) each time the behavior occurs. Specific concrete rewards are given when a predetermined number of tokens is reached (e.g., a new notebook or a pizza for a week's devotions, a new concordance for a month, etc.).

Shaping. Initially, rewards should be frequent, and given for small improvements in behavior. Very gradually the standard is raised so that the goal is reached in gradual increments (shaping). Although the goal may be thirty minutes or more of devotional time per day, the behavior should be shaped towards the goal very gradually, beginning at a minimal level. In general, one cannot begin too low or increase too slowly.

118

The cognitive component. The role of cognitive or mental events (thinking and imaging) must not be overlooked in a plan for behavior change. As noted above, cognitions may substitute for more tangible rewards--at least temporarily. In the form of self-instructions they can also bridge the gap that may exist between antecedent conditions and the desired behavior. For example, through imagined rehearsal (a very potent cognitive aid) an association may be formed between the alarm clock bell and the self-instructions "I must get up and move to the study for devotions," so that when the alarm bell rings the self-instructions occur and the behavior follows. In fact the complete sequence can be strengthened through imagined rehearsal, especially when imagined reward is included.

Other behaviors. In the interests of simplicity a single overt behavior (personal devotions) has been used as an example. However, the same principles may be applied to covert behaviors such as thinking. Thinking on "good things" (Phil. 4:8) or making oneself aware of the presence of God (cf. Brother Lawrence) may be linked to the control of antecedent conditions (I know those who have used the hourly "beep" of an electronic watch with some success). In this case the natural consequences alone may be sufficiently rewarding to maintain the behavior.

More complex behavior, for example loving one's spouse, must be analyzed in terms of the component thoughts and behaviors which would combine to demonstrate that love. As Fromm (1956) has noted, loving is not primarily a feeling over which we have no control, but may be more accurately seen as an "art" or skill which requires effort, and may be modified. Although behavior often follows feelings, feelings may also follow behavior. Love grows from loving actions probably more than we realize.

Cognitive psychology has shown the powerful effect on our lives of keeping in mind an image or "mental picture." We gradually become the thing we picture--either good or bad. Apart from God the natural inclination of man is to set his mind upon the "creature rather than the Creator" (Rom. 1:25).

119

Christ was revealed as the perfect image and likeness of God so that as Christians we may be helped, by keeping Him in view, reflecting upon Him, to gradually be changed into His likeness (Rom. 8:29, II Cor. 3:18). We become like the things we love.

HABITS: A VALUABLE ALLY

We are forming habits whether we wish to or not. If they are not desirable habits they are undesirable. Good habits may be viewed as the necessary groundwork or foundation upon which the spiritual superstructure may rest. The spiritual rewards follow, but the groundwork must be laid. As Brother Lawrence says, "That in the beginning of the spiritual life we ought to be faithful in doing our duty and denying ourselves; but after that, unspeakable pleasures followed." (23) and later, "...by often repeating these acts, they become habitual, and the presence of God rendered as it were natural to us" (34). And finally, "And how can we often think of Him but by a holy habit which we should form of it?" (54) (italics added). The emphasis here is clearly on the individual's part in establishing habits which then become a channel for God's blessing.[1]

Although we frequently admit we are "creatures of habit," too often we use this as an excuse rather than recognizing the opportunities for self-control which are contained in this statement. Too often when self-control is sought it is through an effort of the will; when will-power fails guilt and defeat result. Cognitive behavioral psychology offers an efficient commonsense aid to self-control. Its development serves as a timely reminder to Christians of the importance of habits in their lives.

In summary, we have seen that not only is there reason to accept the relevance of animal studies for humans, but also there is potentially great value in

---

[1] We have been focussing on legitimate human control of habits. For a helpful discussion of the assistance of the Holy Spirit in changing habits see "The Spirit-controlled temperment" or "Transformed temperments" by Tim LaHaye.

doing so. Information gleaned from animal studies of operant and classical conditioning, supplemented with principles of cognitive psychology where appropriate, constitute a powerful tool for change.

The principles of behavior are part of the God-ordained lawfulness in the universe. Although God may intervene miraculously to change behaviors and personalities instantaneously, He has also ordained certain principles by which behavior patterns are established and by which they may be modified systematically. Although in many cases these are implicit in Scripture, at times they are explicit; for example, the importance of practice ("Train up a child in the way he should go..." Prov. 22:6), the effect of cognitions or thought on behavior ("...for as he thinketh in his heart, so is he." Prov. 23:7), the negative influence of environmental stimuli, or behavioral antecedents ("...do not proceed in the way of evil men. Avoid it, do not pass by it;" Prov. 4:15), and the influence of consequences or rewards on behavior ("By faith Moses, ...refused to be called the son of Pharoah's daughter... for he was looking to the reward," Heb. 11:24, 26, "Rejoice, and be glad, for your reward in heaven is great...," Matt. 5:12). In addition, behavior itself is emphasized both as evidence of the spiritual ("...show me your faith without the works, and I will show you my faith by my works." James 2:18), and even as a determinant of the spiritual ("Where your treasure is, there will your heart be also." Matt. 6:21).

DISCUSSION QUESTIONS

In our discussion so far we have outlined some reasons for a limited acceptance of animal-based learning principles. In this area as in others, a simpler solution would be either complete acceptance or complete rejection. However, an honest appraisal usually does not allow this "simpler solution." As is often the case, the task of thoughtful Christians is to sort the wheat from the chaff. This also is the basic task in the first two of the following issues noted briefly below.

Free will. Christians, especially North American evangelicals, have typically placed a very strong emphasis on the capacity of the individual for free choice. As we noted above this is a major reason for the negative reaction many Christians have towards the complete determinism associated with learning explanations of behavior. We have argued that free will is often voluntarily subjected to environmental control as habits are acquired, although we suggested that choice of habits is always possible ("reciprocal determinism"). Is this the thin edge of the wedge leading ultimately to acceptance of determinism as psychologists discover more and more of the environmental factors which control our behavior?

Assuming that God is behind all of the cause-effect relationships which constitute our environment, and discovering the influence of that environment upon us, will we be led ultimately to a "Christian determinism" (a kind of "environmentally mediated predestination")? Once again the question is where to draw the line.

Reward vs. punishment. Our discussion has focussed primarily on the influence of rewards on behavior. This was done to simplify the discussion and to reflect the main interest of Skinner and other researchers in this area. Skinner argues that rewarding desired behavior is not only more pleasant for the learner, but also more efficient in changing the behavior than is punishment. At best punishment is said to inhibit the punished response in the punished situation without teaching a desirable alternative. It also models a negative aggressive behavior. However, recently Balsam and Bondy (1983), have argued that even rewards may have negative side effects.

Perhaps we can learn something from Skinner that will make our homes, schools, and prisons more pleasant. But is reward the answer? Or for that matter is punishment? Certainly we need to explore these issues, and perhaps again the question is one of balance
.

Language. As a Christian I am pleased to see in psychology the resurgence of interest in studying some of what Koteskey (1980) calls man's "God-like" characteristics, creativity, imagery, and particularly language.

The use of words is extremely important in Scripture. God spoke the creation into existence; Jesus is called the "Word"; the significance of Babel and Pentecost are closely linked to the importance of language; and there is great power associated with an individual's name. In addition, Christians have usually considered the ability to communicate with words to be part of the image of God in man.

However, recently several researchers claim to have taught animals, usually chimpanzees or apes, to communicate through language. Using sign language, blocks, or keyboards and computer-generated voices, the animals have signalled their needs and even generated word combinations (Gardner and Gardner, 1972; Rumbaugh, 1977; Patterson, 1978).

But is this truly language? There is no doubt that the animals are using symbols as signs to stand for objects and actions. However, there are significant questions being raised about the comparison with human language (Slobin, 1979; Seidenberg and Petitto, 1979).

Christians need to think carefully about what they mean when they talk about the image of God in man. The area of human learning and psycholinguistics offers some intriguing questions for thoughtful Christians. What is the origin of human speech--is it learned (Skinner, 1957) or largely innate (Chomsky, 1968, 1969)? Is human speech unique? Do the studies of language in animals necessitate a redefinition of the uniqueness of man?

Artificial intelligence. Some of the same questions arise with regard to attempts to create machines in man's image--computers having the ability to think like humans (artificial intelligence, or simply AI). Computers can talk and they can respond to the human voice. Psychologists and linguists are making great strides in developing the ability in computers to "think" (e.g., to learn from mistakes, to have imagination, and even "common sense"). Will they achieve their goal? If they do what will it mean for man's view of himself as unique, and the Christian's view of him as created in God's image? As Emerson and Forbes (1984) suggest these are significant questions which AI raises for contemporary Christians.

In conclusion, we have seen that the area of "learning and cognition" contains some difficult questions, as well as some valuable aids for Christians. Here, as elsewhere, the decisions to accept or reject various positions have important implications for a Christian view of man. These decisions are ones in which every Christian interested in the relationship between psychology and Christianity has both a stake and a contribution to make.

SUGGESTED READINGS

Cosgrove, M. 1982. B.F. Skinner's behaviorism: An analysis. Grand Rapids: Zondervan. Clear analysis of Skinner's radical position, considering basic assumptions and their relationship to Christian assumptions, as well as values and limitations of this approach.

Dobson, James. 1970. Dare to discipline. Wheaton, IL: Tyndale. Very practical and helpful child-rearing book by a popular, knowledgeable, Christian author. Interesting here because of its extensive use of behavioral techniques.

Emerson, A. & Forbes, C. 1984. Living in a world with thinking machines. Christianity Today, 28, 2, 14-18. Thought provoking article on the challenge of AI for a Christian view of man, which sometimes tends to be bevioristic.

Ratcliff, D.E. 1978. Using behavioral psychology to encourage personal evangelism. Journal of Psychology and Theology, 6, 219-224. Interesting practical application of behavioral principles to a Christian concern.

Schaeffer, F. 1972. Back to freedom and dignity. Downers Grove, IL: InterVarsity Press. Helpful analysis and discussion of Skinner's controversial book, together with a clear Christian response.

Skinner, B.F. 1971. Beyond freedom and dignity. New York: Bantam Books. The logical and consistent conclusion to radical behaviorism--

freedom and dignity are harmful illusions. A best-seller; it will make you think.

REFERENCES AND OTHER SOURCES

Adams, J.E. 1973. The Christian counselor's manual. Grand Rapids: Baker Book House.

Balsam, P.D., & Bondy, A.S. 1983. The negative side effects of reward. Journal of Applied Behavior Analysis, 16, 283-296.

Beck, A. & Greenberg, R.L. 1974. Coping with depression. New York: Institute for Rational Living.

Boivrin, M.J. 1985. Behavioral Psychology: What does it have to offer the Christian Church? Journal of the American Scientific Affiliation,, 37, 79-85.

Bower, G. & Bower, S. 1978. Asserting yourself: A practical guide for positive change. Reading, Mass.: Addison-Wesley.

Brother Lawrence. 1958. The practice of the presence of God. Old Tappan, NJ.: Fleming H. Revell.

Chomsky, N. 1968. Language and the mind. New York: Harcourt Brace Jovanovich.

Chomsky, N. 1969. Language and the mind. Readings in psychology today. Del Mar, CA: CRM Books.

Cosgrove, M. 1982. B.F. Skinner's behaviorism: An analysis. Grand Rapids: Zondervan.

Danaher, B. & Lichtenstein, E. 1978. Become an ex-smoker. Englewood Cliffs, N.J.: Prentice-Hall.

Dobson, James. 1970. Dare to discipline. Wheaton, IL: Tyndale.

Emerson, A. & Forbes, C. 1984. Living in a world with thinking machines. Christianity Today, 28, 2, 14-18.

Festinger, L. 1964. Behavioral support for opinion change. Public Opinion Quarterly, 28, 404-417.

Fromm, Eric. 1956. The art of loving. New York: Harper.

Gardner, B.T. & Gardner, R.A. 1972. Two-way communication with an infant chimpanzee. In Schrier, A.M., & Stollnitz, F., (Eds.) Behavior of nonhuman primates, Vol. 4 New York: Academic Press.

James, William. 1900. Psychology: Briefer course. New York: Henry Holt & Co.

Koteskey, R.L. 1980. Psychology from a Christian perspective. Nashville: Abingdon.

Koteskey, R.L. 1983. General psychology for Christian counselors. Nashville: Abingdon.

Lakein, A. 1974. How to get control of your time and your life. New York: New World Library.

Myers, D.G. 1983. Social psychology. New York: McGraw-Hill.

Miller, W. & Munoz, R. 1976. How to control your drinking. Englewood Cliffs, N.J.: Prentice-Hall.

Patterson, G. & Gullion, E. 1971. Living with children: New methods for parents and teachers. Champaign, Ill.: Research Press.

Patterson, F.G. 1978. The gestures of a gorilla: Language acquisition in another pongid. Brain and Language, 5, 72-97.

Ratcliff, D.E. 1978. Using behavioral psychology to encourage personal evangelism. Journal of Psychology and Theology, 6, 219-224.

Robinson, F. 1970. Effective study, (4th ed.). New York: Harper & Row.

Rumbaugh, D.M. 1977. An introduction to human information processing. New York: Wiley.

Schaeffer, F. 1972. Back to freedom and dignity. Downers Grove, IL: InterVarsity Press.

Seidenberg, M.S., & Petitto, L.A. 1979. Signing behavior in apes. Cognition, 7, 177-215.

Skinner, B.F. 1957. Verbal behavior. New York; Appleton-Century-Crofts.

Skinner, B.F. 1971. Beyond freedom and dignity. New York: Bantam Books.

Slobin, D.I. 1979. Psycholinguistics (2nd. ed.). Glenville, IL: Scott, Foresman.

Stuart, R. & Davis, B. 1972. Slim chance in a fat world. Champaign, Ill.: Research Press.

Watson, D. & Tharp, R. 1981. Self-directed behavior: Self-modification for personal adjustment. Monterey: Brooks/Cole.

Williams, R. & Long, J. 1979. Toward a self-managed life-style. Boston: Houghton Mifflin Company.

CHAPTER 7:
PERSONALITY THEORY

"**N**ow tell me a bit about yourself, Martin," asked Dr. Fringers as he leaned back in his chair.

"Well I think I'm a competent, aggressive person who basically knows what he wants and sets out to get it. After receiving my masters degree in business administration I went to work for Atlas Forest Products. When I wasn't advancing as quickly as I wanted I found a better position with Zeigler Developments. I was married for a while but we were crowding each other so we went our own ways. I've had a couple of temporary relationships since then but nothing at the moment. I have a townhouse in Market Gardens and a condo at Big Star where I ski. I play racquetball twice a week, go out for dinner often, drive a new car, travel a lot, and basically do what ever I want--but somehow I'm not happy. I know I should be but I'm not. I look at other people around me and they seem happy, but I just seem to get more and more depressed."

PERSONALITY THEORY

What is Martin's problem? Did he suffer childhood trauma or frustration? Is his environmental conditioning at fault? Has he been frustrated in his attempt to develop to his full potential? Is he simply a spoiled 20th Century "Yuppie," a sinner suffering pangs of guilt?

The way that you answer these questions reveals something about your own "theory of personality." Each of us holds certain beliefs about why people behave as they do. For example, "people are basically honest," or "people are basically sinful," or "like father like son." Taken together these beliefs make up our view of other people and human nature in general. Most of us do not spell out our views of human nature in organized detail. Nevertheless these views make up what psychologists call our "implicit theories of personality," and they determine the way we act and react towards other people.

Psychologists interested in constructing an organized explanation for all human behavior make their views explicit in carefully developed "theories of personality." Usually these theories are associated with a particular form of therapy. However, our concern here is with different ways of understanding human nature; therapy will be discussed further in Chapter 9.

The first fully developed theory of personality, the "psychoanalytic theory," was developed by Sigmund Freud in the first few decades of this century. Freud believed that human behavior was controlled by basic drives and instincts. He also believed that the pattern for our behavior (our personality) was set very early in life, and that we are not aware of most of the reasons for the things we think and do. If our young friend Martin visited a Freudian analyst his drive for pleasure and conspicuous consumption might be traced to either frustration or over-indulgence in feeding during the early months of his life, which led to a "fixation" of sexual energy at this stage of development. The analyst would look for signs of unconscious frustration and anger as a cause of his depression.

During the second quarter of this century the most popular approach within psychology generally was a rigidly scientific behaviorism. This gave rise to a very different approach to personality developed by B.F. Skinner. Skinner believes that all of our patterns of behavior (our personality) are learned from rewards and punishments in our surrounding environment. He believes that in this way our environment **completely** controls us. If Martin visited a Skinnerian "behavior therapist" the therapist would attempt to understand Martin's unhappiness as the result of habits of responding which were bringing Martin too much punishment and not enough reward.

In the last two or three decades both psychoanalysis and behavior therapy have stimulated the reaction of a "third force" in psychology called "humanistic psychology."[1]

---

[1] More recently "Transpersonal psychology" has emerged claiming to be a "fourth force". Transpersonal psychology is a further development of humanist psychology with a greater interest in Eastern religions and mysticism (cf. Tart, 1975). Although its claim to be a "fourth force" is somewhat exaggerated, it does

Humanistic psychologists, such as Carl Rogers, do not agree with Freud that people are like a animals (instinctual, irrational, and determined), or with Skinner that they are like machines (programmed and controlled). They are critical of the low view of human nature taken by the earlier two movements and proclaim a much higher view. If Martin visited a humanistic psychologist, his difficulties might be seen as the result of restrictive relationships which had produced a "lack of congruence" between his self-concept and his true self. This prevented him from growing into his naturally good, beautiful, and happy self.

Each of these three major approaches (there are many variations of each, as well as some others which are difficult to categorize) is a well developed theory of human personality and human behavior, although each makes very different basic assumptions about the nature of the person. Each has waxed as its influential leaders developed ideas current in the culture; psychoanalysis and behavior therapy have waned as the culture changed and their leaders either died or faded from the scene. Because humanistic psychology is the most recent and currently popular major theoretical approach we will consider it in greater detail. It has also had perhaps the greatest impact on the North American Christian church. This impact, although often very subtle, has at times provoked strong criticism.[1]

EVALUATING THEORIES

Before considering humanistic psychology further, it will be helpful to consider the question of how a Christian might evaluate a theory of personality. We are not concerned here with the usual standards by which theories are evaluated (parsimony, elegance, etc.). Rather we are concerned with the unique questions which a Christian might ask of a theory.

---

appear to be a bridge from psychology to the controversial "New Age" movement. For a balanced discussion of this movement, with additional references, see Burrows (1986); Groothuis, (1986).

[1]   For example see Hinman, 1980; Kilpatrick, 1983, 1985; Vitz, 1977.

Most major theories of personality were developed by non-Christians. Some of these, such as Skinner and Rogers, had merely rejected Christianity early in their lives, and some, such as Freud, were openly critical of, and antagonistic to, Christianity. Nevertheless, the character and beliefs of the founder are inadequate grounds on which to evaluate a theory (we benefit from mechanical and electronic devices everyday which were developed by non-Christians).

Sometimes theories are accepted or rejected on the basis of their effectiveness. If the theory leads to a form of therapy which seems to work it may be accepted on those grounds as in some sense "true." This too is inadequate as the sole indication of acceptability.[1] A theory may "work" for the wrong reasons. It may be accurate in one small way but entirely inaccurate in others.

The primary concern of the Christian should be not "Was the founder a Christian?" or "Does it work?" but "Is it compatible with basic Christian belief?" This means we must examine the **assumptions** upon which the theory has been developed, to see whether or not they agree with our Christian assumptions. Some basic Christian assumptions about the human being include the following (from Sire, 1976, pp. 29-35):

1. Humans are created in the image of God and thus possess personality, self-transcendence, intelligence, morality, gregariousness and creativity.

2. God can and does communicate with humans.

3. Humans were created good, but through the Fall the image of God became defaced, though not so ruined as not to be capable of restoration; through the work of Christ God redeemed humanity and began the process of restoring it to goodness, though any given person may choose to reject that redemption.

---

[1]. A possible exception is the situation where the theory is merely "used" and is never taken to reflect "reality" in any sense. See our discussion of "instrumentalism" in Chapter 9.

Of course this list could be extended and elaborated greatly. The point here is that there are some pretty basic and important Christian assumptions on the nature of the person, and that these are the criteria by which a theory should be evaluated.[1]

This approach to evaluation is frequently difficult since personality theorists often do not spell out their assumptions. However, secondary sources, textbooks on personality theory, are usually helpful here.[2]

Let us now return to our consideration of humanistic psychology and see what effect basic assumptions have.

HUMANISTIC THEORY OF PERSONALITY

Like other movements within psychology, humanistic psychology developed as a reaction to earlier approaches, primarily psychoanalysis and behaviorism. Whereas the psychoanalyst sees people as seething cauldrons of forces determined by instincts and unconscious conflicts, and the behaviorist sees them as controlled by their environment, and both see people as no better than complex animals, to the humanist they are much more. Humans are unique beings, with dignity and intrinsic worth. They are not under the power of either their instincts or their environment but have the ability to overcome these and make meaningful choices.

Humanistic psychology has several things within it to commend it to Christians. First, it asserts that humans are not completely controlled (determined) by either their past, their heredity, or their environment, but possess the power of choice. Christianity, too, assumes that we have been given the responsibility of meaningful

---

[1]. More complete discussions may be found in Evans, 1977, p. 142 ff.; as well as Sire, 1976, p. 20 ff. See also the "Christian Humanist Manifesto" contained in an article titled "Secular vs. Christian Humanism" in Eternity Magazine, January 1982, pp. 16-18.

[2] A clear approach of this type is taken by Hjelle and Ziegler, 1981.

choices--from Adam and Eve in the garden to individual responsiveness to Jesus Christ. Second, humanistic psychology affirms the dignity and worth of the person as a unique being distinct from animals. Christianity also is clear in its belief that the person occupies a unique position in creation--the image bearer of God. For these reasons Christians have found humanistic psychology a valuable ally in their opposition to certain tenets of psychoanalytic and behaviorist views of humanity.

However, beyond unique, valuable, and free, the humanist asserts that humanity is good, and here the paths begin to diverge. Carl Rogers' view is particularly optimistic (1951, 1957, 1961). He likens each of us to the seed of a flower waiting to sprout and unfold in all its beauty (discounting the possibility that the seed may produce a noxius weed). He believes we have within us a strong natural drive to develop ("actualize") all of our potential. Given the right environment, that is, one in which we are fully accepted, we will naturally develop into the beautiful person whose potential we carry within. Problems arise when parents and others impose conditions upon their acceptance of us. That is, they say or imply that they will accept and love us if we behave as they want us to. This leads us to distort our true nature and fail to develop as we might otherwise (which, it is assumed, would have been much better). The drive to "actualize" our true selves remains however, so that if an environment of complete acceptance can be found (i.e., as in therapy) we will once again begin to grow.

In their view of human nature and society generally, the humanist psychologists are irrepressible optimists. To them, not only is the natural state of humanity good, but conflicts between people are not at all inevitable, being merely the result of distortions of their basically good nature.

Because of this assumption of the innate goodness of humanity, many Christians see humanistic psychology in complete opposition to Christianity. There has been no dearth of Christian writers ready to "unmask humanistic psychology for the hoax it really is" (Tim La Haye, quoted in Hinman, 1980). On the other hand, in the absence of a thoroughly developed and well articulated Christian theory of personality, many Christians have attempted to adapt the humanistic theories of Carl Rogers for their own use. The primary modification, of course, is in the view of the innate goodness of the individual.

To the evangelical Christian the Bible is very clear that humanity is "fallen" and sinful, and that wars and fighting are the inevitable consequence of internal conflict (for this reason many Christians find Freud's views closer to their own). However, changing this basic assumption of Rogers' theory raises some new questions.

CONTROVERSIAL ISSUE

One of the most important questions raised concerns our attitude towards ourselves. If we are (a) free, (b) unique and valuable, but (c) inherently evil, the humanistic attitude of simple optimism is no longer satisfactory. The fundamental position of complete acceptance towards self and others is called into question if these "selves" are not basically good. In an attempt to get a better perspective on this problem we will consider the following question:

Should I love myself, or hate myself?

Much of the Christian opposition to humanistic psychology has focussed on its promotion of "love of self," derived from the assumption of the individual's basic goodness. The Christian position, which views the person as the fallen image of God, is more complex. By delineating a biblical attitude to "self" we will be able to observe some of the changes necessary when a basic assumption of a personality theory is changed.

Hate myself. A biblical view of humans must clearly acknowledge their basic sinfulness and propensity for evil. From the womb they go astray continually (Ps. 58:3). Their hearts are deceitful

134

and wicked (Jer. 17:9). Even their righteousness is "like a filthy garment" (Isa. 64:6). It is not hard for some Christians to see humans as worthless, despicable "worms."

Even after acknowledging his or her sin a person is told to "deny himself (or herself), and take up his (her) cross"--clearly a message of self-abnegation. Christian psychologist Bruce Narramore quotes spiritual life author Roy Hession saying that Jesus saw us to be"...worms having forfeited all rights by our sin, except to deserve hell. And now calls us to take our rightful place as worms for Him and with Him" (Narramore, 1984, p.136). Thus a sinful worm becomes a "worm for Jesus," but a worm nevertheless.

This negative view of human nature finds support in other areas as well. There is ample evidence in any news broadcast of the practical consequences of an evil nature--theft, murder, rape. Freud's conclusion, after a lifetime of careful study, was that conflict and war were the natural products of our very psyches. Finally, if this is not enough, honest self-examination reveals abundant cause for dismay. Thus, from the in-depth analyses of astute observers such as Freud, to the events on the evening news, to observation of our own thoughts, the conclusion is inescapable: there is a great deal to hate in human nature.

Furthermore, the love of self is the very root of sin. In fact one of the signs of the last days is that "men will be lovers of self" (II Tim. 3:2). The command to love our neighbor as ourselves is not to be understood as an injunction to love ourselves but rather to love our neighbor **as in fact we already do love ourselves.** Self-love is admitted not commanded.

But must I go around hating myself, continually putting myself down? Is this not in fact a major component of mental illness?

Love myself. In seeming contrast to the above position, there are numerous Scriptures that affirm our worth. Bruce Narramore outlines them in the following way:

1. We are created in the image of God (Gen. 1:26, 27, and I Cor. 11:7).
2. We are the apex of God's creative actions (Gen. 1 and 2).
3. We are given dominion over the earth (Gen. 1:28-30).
4. We are told that we are made a little lower than the angels and crowned with glory and honor (Ps. 8:4-6).
5. We were purchased out of sin by Christ's death (1 Pet. 1:18, 19).
6. We are indwelled by the Holy Spirit (Eph. 1:13).
7. We have eternity prepared for us (Jn. 14:1-3). (Narramore, 1984, p. 141)

He then quotes Francis Schaeffer who says,

> I am convinced that one of the great weaknesses in evangelical preaching in the last few years is that we have lost sight of the biblical fact that man is wonderful. We have seen the unbiblical humanism which surrounds us, and, to resist this in our emphasis on man's lostness, we have tended to reduce man to a zero. Man is indeed lost, but that does not mean that he is nothing. We must resist humanism, but to make man a zero is neither the right way nor the best way to resist it. You can emphasize that man is totally lost and still have the biblical answer that man is really great.

Here then is the paradox--"man is totally lost," but also "really great." Narrow acceptance of one truth without acknowledging the other leads to either premature rejection or naive acceptance of humanist psychology.

The resolution of this paradox is found in a recognition that we are a complex composite of good and evil, having by the grace of God, an awareness and desire for good, yet continually failing in our efforts for good (Rom. 7:19). Although clouded or defaced, the image of God remains, and thus, however faulty, our sense of moral obligation, our rationality, our creativity, our aesthetic appreciation, etc. These are "God-like" characteristics, to use Koteskey's (1980)

136

term, and must be affirmed. On the other hand, the consequences of the fall, our moral depravity, selfishness, malice, refusal to worship God, are not to be affirmed but repudiated entirely.

In this area Clark (1985) makes a useful distinction using the words "worthy" and "worthful." He points out that although we are not "worthy" we nevertheless have worth--we are "worthful." Scripture makes it clear that not deserving salvation, we nevertheless are worth saving. Just as a lost pirate treasure does not create in its salvagers a moral obligation to salvage it, although once it is salvaged it may have great value, so too our lost state does not create in God any obligation to save us, but He still sees in us tremendous worth, and at great cost to Himself, saves us. Though not worthy we are worthful.

How are we to answer our question then? Should I love myself or hate myself?

Apparently the answer is not simple. For one thing the word self-love is ambiguous. Even outside the Christian context it may refer to attitudes from self-respect to narcissism. Self-love is bad when it is excessive, leads to comparison with others, self-deification, and an obsession with self. This "bad" self-love is obvious in arrogance. It is less apparent but equally dangerous in the inferiority complex based upon selfish and self-centered self-condemnation. On the other hand the appropriate level of self-love, which seems to be assumed in Scripture as the basis for loving others, leads to an appreciation for God's image, and a legitimate self-respect.

This self-love however, is never obvious in and of itself, but underlies other more noticeable characteristics. It may show itself as a genuine concern for others and an actual **forgetfulness** of self. It may need to become the object of attention in prayer and therapy in certain conditions where a poor view of self interferes with the ability to help others, but in most cases it is adequate and may be assumed and accepted.

To summarize, we are "unworthy" but "worthful," and may love those characteristics which give us "worth" in God's sight, being

137

created in His image, and hate those tendencies which are contrary, especially the tendency to try to make ourselves "worthy." The love we have for ourselves is generally not something we need to encourage but rather accept. The hate needs to be focussed on those parts of our nature which echo the fall and continue to drive a wedge between us and God.

CHRISTIAN HUMANISM

We noted earlier that there are aspects of humanistic psychology which commend it to Christians. One important reservation we had was the assumption that humans are basically good, and the related idea that we should love ourselves. Having discussed the idea that a certain kind and amount of self-love is appropriate, on the basis of an "unworthy" but "worthful" view of the person, let us consider what this might mean for a Christian view of humanistic psychology generally.

First, a Christian view of personality recognizes that humans are of tremendous worth, having been created by God in His own image, and although fallen, nevertheless considered by God to be worth saving. In fact, J. I. Packer and Thomas Howard, in their book Christianity: The true humanism (1985), point out that only Christianity gives a valid basis for assuming humans have value. Therefore let us not abandon the word "humanism," but follow Packer and Howard in distinguishing between secular and Christian humanism, the latter affirming that "The proper study of mankind is not man alone, but God and man together."[1]

Second, as we noted earlier, there is a great deal within humanity that is not lovely. Therefore, the Christian humanist psychologist cannot promote the natural development of all the inborn tendencies within an individual. Many of these are harmful, not only to others, but to the individual himself or herself. From a Christian perspective the goal of development is not whatever comes forth when all

---

[1] Part of the "Christian Humanist Manifesto" reprinted by Packer and Howard, pp. 239-242, from an article titled "Secular vs. Christian Humanism" in Eternity Magazine, January 1982, pp. 16-18.

138

restrictions are removed, but rather a guided growth, including pruning where necessary, into "Christ-likeness."

The consequence of this very important deviation from secular humanist psychology is that while both the Christian therapist and the non-Christian Rogerian therapist must show "unconditional positive regard" for the **person**, he or she has a different view of undesirable thoughts and behavior. The Rogerian therapist, while he or she may object to certain thoughts and behaviors in me as a client, can only do so if my thoughts and behaviors are inconsistent with my self-structure. If I recognize my sadistic behavior for what it is, and this is consistent with my consciously perceived self, the therapist cannot object (cf. Roberts, 1985). The Christian therapist on the other hand, accepts outside criteria (e.g., Scripture, the authority of the church), as legitimate standards by which to evaluate his or her client. Some of the client's thoughts and behaviors may be blatantly wrong (sinful) and consequently harmful. Correction is then required. God loves us regardless of what we have done, but only forgives us if we repent. This is very different from secular humanism.

Similarly on a personal level, the Christian individual can love and accept himself or herself as a person of worth, while at the same time confessing, disciplining, and controlling his or her un-Christlike tendencies.

To summarize, a Christian humanist view of personality asserts that humans are not completely controlled by their past, their heredity, or their environment, but possesses a significant degree of freedom (and therefore responsibility), and that being a composite of good and evil, they are worthy of unconditional love as individuals, yet require discipline and correction in order to develop to their fullest potential, which is to be like Christ.

Thus a Christian humanist view of the person has in common with the secular view a respect for his or her freedom, uniqueness, and worth. It does not accept the secular position on his or her basic goodness, but distinguishes between good and evil tendencies. The implications of this position for our love for ourselves were noted above. We will discuss further the implications for therapy in Chapter 9.

DISCUSSION QUESTIONS

The area of personality theory has many other potentially controversial issues. Each secular theory raises new questions. The approach illustrated above, that of examining basic assumptions, is a fruitful way of evaluating any theory of personality. However, there are several other issues which a Christian may encounter in the study of personality. Some of these are outlined below.

What is the "spirit"? The Bible uses many terms to refer to the "parts" of the individual. These have been variously translated as "body," "soul," "spirit," "heart," "bowels," "mind," etc. Psychologists studying personality also refer to different "parts" of the individual, using such terms as "body," "mind," "self," "psyche," "id," "ego," "superego," "unconscious."[1] Do all these terms refer to different "parts" of the individual which are distinct but interacting, or are they just a way of emphasizing different aspects or characteristics of the same total person? For example, when a psychologist studies "consciousness," (or to use the older terms, the "mind," "soul," or "psyche") is the psychologist studying that part of us which will survive death and live forever? Or is that another totally different part--the "spirit"

In a letter to his mother a Royal Air Force Squadron Pilot (WW II) says: "We are sent to this world to acquire a personality and a character to take with us that can never be taken from us." How accurate is this statement? Does the

---

[1] Tim LaHaye in his popular books "Spirit-controlled Temperment" and "Transformed Temperments" distinguishes between temperment (traits we are born with), character (emotions, will, mind, or soul), and personality (the facade we show to others). His approach, based on the ancient Greek theory of body humors, emphasizes the power of the Holy Spirit to modify inherited characteristics.

140

personality represent those enduring characteristics which will survive death and by which we will be known. Is the "spirit" more closely allied to the **total personality**?

What is the "spirit," and how is it related to the structure of personality?

Psychoanalytic theory. We have emphasized humanistic personality theory in our discussion above. However, many Christians find the theories of Sigmund Freud to be more readily adapted to their Christian perspective. Within psychoanalytic personality theory there appears to be at least a superficial similarity between a Christian view of the individual and the view of personality structure originally proposed by Freud (although similar ideas may be traced back to Plato and Socrates): the individual's sinful fallen nature, the "flesh," is like the "id"; his or her "soul" or "mind" is like the "ego"; and the "conscience" and perhaps the "spirit" are like the "superego."[1] How far can this analogy be accepted? What are the implications of substituting Christian assumptions for non-Christian assumptions in Freud's theory? Where must Christians part company with Freud?

Sex and religion. It is well known that Freud (1920) saw the sex drive ("Eros") as one of two primary motivators of human behavior (the other being "Thanatos" or death). He claimed it is responsible not only for procreation but through redirection ("sublimation") for all of humanity's highest achievements, including religion. Historically sexual activity and religious behavior have frequently been linked in the form of temple prostitutes, and various alluring deities on the one hand, and sexual abstinence and virginity on the other. The contemporary religious scene is not without its own evidence as all too frequently the more ardent, and zealous religious leaders fall prey to sexual sins, suggesting a mis-direction of the same powerful drive. Christian psychologists Phyllis Hart (1984) and Harold Ellens (1984) have both suggested that there is a close association

---

[1] Other similarities have been noted in Chapter 4 and by the authors cited there, especially Vitz and Gartner. See Chapter 1 in Meier et al for a possible historical link between Freud's ideas and Romans 7.

between sexuality and spirituality which may be traced to a common life force. A further consideration is the Bible's comparison of the husband-wife relationship to the Christ-church relationship (cf. I Cor. 6:15-20; Eph. 5:21-33).

A Christian view of personality must take account of this (these) basic drive(s). What is the relationship between sexuality and spirituality? Are they completely unrelated, perhaps antagonistic drives, or are they two different manifestations of a single "life force"?

Testing. Psychologists studying personality have developed a wide variety of tests to measure different personality traits. These range from "projective" tests such as the well-known Rorschach ink-blot, to simple "yes" or "no" answers on paper and pencil scales. In addition several attempts have been made to develop measures of "religiousness." A particularly interesting approach is presented in an article titled "The Shepherd scale: Separating the sheep from the goats" (Bassett et.al., 1981).[1] Do any of these tap spiritual maturity? Could a separate scale of spiritual maturity be developed?

In conclusion, there is no widely held and clearly articulated Christian theory of personality. When Christian assumptions are applied to secular theories often extensive reorganization is necessary (as we saw with humanistic theory when the assumption of humanity's goodness was changed). In earlier chapters we noted some Christian use of behavioristic theory (Chapter 6) and psychoanalytic theory (Chapter 4) and we will discuss further applications of these and other approaches in Chapter 9. However, despite the fact that many Christians use techniques based on these theories, there remains a very great void in the realm of Christian theorizing. A Christian theory of personality based upon a biblical view of the nature of the person remains one of the greatest needs in contemporary Christian psychology. As we turn to a consideration of psychopathology (Chapter 8) and psychotherapy (Chapter 9), the

---

[1] For a good discussion of the measurement of religiousness see Meadow and Kahoe, 1984, pp. 300-314.

142

central nature of this need will become even more
apparent.

SUGGESTED READINGS

Clark, D.K. 1985. Philosophical reflections on
self-worth and self-love. Journal of
Psychology and Theology, 13, 3-11. Clear
helpful discussion of self-love. Presents
balanced view of "unworthy" but "worthful."

Kilpatrick, W. 1985. The emperor's new clothes:
The naked truth about psychology. Crossway
Books. One of the most recent of the many
books criticizing humanistic psychology.
Notable primarily because of the popularity
and wide exposure of this theme.

Packer, J.I., & Howard, T. 1985. Christianity: The
true humanism. Waco, TX: Word. An excellent
work by articulate Christians. Scholarly yet
readable analysis of humanism and its origins
in Christianity. Draws an important
distinction between secular and Christian
humanism. Highly recommended for informed
discussion on humanism.

Roberts, R.C. 1985, November. Therapy for the
saints: Does empathy equal Christian love?
Christianity Today, pp. 25-28. Clear, concise
presentation of some important differences
between Client-centered therapy and a biblical
approach.

Sire, J. 1976. The universe next door. Downers
Grove: InterVarsity Press. A very useful
analysis of "world views" for the layman.
Presents fundamental Christian assumptions
and shows how these are dealt with by various
other world views.

REFERENCES AND OTHER SOURCES

Bassett, R.L., Sadler, R.D., Kobischen, E.E.,
Skiff, D.M., Merill, I.J., Atwater, B.J., and
Livermore, P.W. 1981. The Shepherd scale:
Separating the sheep from the goats. Journal
of Psychology and Theology, 9, 335-351.

143

Brownback, P. 1982. The danger of self love. Chicago: Moody Press.

Clark, D.K. 1985. Philosophical reflections on self-worth and self-love. Journal of Psychology and Theology, 13, 3-11.

Ellens, J.H. 1984. Psychology in worship. (at press)

Evans, C. 1977. Preserving the person: A look at the human sciences. Downers Grove, IL: InterVarsity Press.

Freud, S. (1920) 1961. Beyond the pleasure principle. New York: W.W. Norton.

Hart, P.P. 1984. Eros: Sexuality and spirituality. Journal of Psychology and Chritianity, 3, 69-74.

Hjelle, L.A. & Ziegler, D.J. 1981. Personality theories: Basic assumptions, research, and applications. New York: McGraw-Hill.

Hinman, N.E. 1980. An answer to humanistic psychology. Irvine, California: Harvest House Publishers.

Kilpatrick, W.K. 1983. Psychological seduction. Nashville, TN: Nelson.

Kilpatrick, W. 1985. The emperor's new clothes: The naked truth about psychology. Crossway Books.

Koteskey, Ronald L. 1980. Psychology from a Christian perspective. Nashville: Abingdon.

LaHaye, T. 1966. The spirit-controlled temperment. Wheaton, IL: Tyndale House.

LaHaye, T. 1971. Transformed temperments. Wheaton, IL: Tyndale House.

McDowell, J. 1984. His image...my image. San Bernardino: Here's Life Publishers.

Meadow, M.J. & Kahoe, R.D. 1984. Psychology of religion: Religion in individual lives. New York: Harper and Row.

Meier, P., Minirth, F., & Wichern, F. 1982. Introduction to psychology and counseling. Grand Rapids, MI: Baker.

Narramore, S. B. 1984. No condemnation. Grand Rapids: Zondervan.

Packer, J.I., & Howard, T. 1985. Christianity: The true humanism. Waco, TX: Word.

Roberts, R.C. 1985. Carl Rogers and the Christian virtues. Journal of Psychology and Theology, 13, 263-273.

Roberts, R.C. 1985, November. Therapy for the saints: Does empathy equal Christian love? Christianity Today, pp. 25-28.

144

Rogers, C. 1951. _Client=centered__therapy:__Its current__practice._implications,__and__theory.._ Boston: Houghton Mifflin.

Rogers, C. 1957. A note on the nature of man. _Journal__of__Counseling__Psychology_, 4, 199-203.

Rogers, C. 1961. _On__becoming__a__person:__A therapist's__view__of__psychotherapy_. Boston: Houghton Mifflin.

Secular vs. Christian Humanism. (1982, January). _Eternity_. pp. 16-18.

Sire, J. 1976. _The__universe__next__door_. Downers Grove: InterVarsity Press.

Stott, J.R.W. 1984, April. Am I supposed to love myself or hate myself? _Christianity__Today_, pp. 26-28.

Vitz, Paul C. 1977. _Psychology__as__religion:__The cult_of_self=worship_. Grand Rapids: Eerdmans.

CHAPTER 8: ABNORMAL PSYCHOLOGY

What are mental disorders?

MENTAL ILLNESS
BEHAVIOR DISORDER
A SIN PROBLEM
DEMON POSSESSION
HOLISTIC APPROACH
DISCUSSION QUESTIONS
    Who is abnormal?
    Homosexuality
    Mental health and the Christian
SUGGESTED READINGS
REFERENCES AND OTHER SOURCES

147

The young man who sat across from my desk looked down at his lap as he mumbled, "Kill them... I'll get a gun and kill them... fall down...down the road. Escape... Friday... He'll see... trees around... Pow Pow... dead." There seemed little doubt that this young man was abnormal, but what was the nature of his difficulty? What had caused it? Had it come on quickly or over a matter of years? What were the chances of improvement? How should he be treated? In short, did his problem belong to a particular "category" of disorders with known causes, symptoms, prognosis, and a prescribed treatment? "Abnormal Psychology" is the specialized field of psychology which attempts to answer these questions.

As we saw in the last chapter, there is a great deal of disagreement among psychologists in the view they take of the nature of the person (theories of personality). These different views lead to very different treatments or therapies as we will see in the next chapter. In this chapter we find that different views of the nature of the person lead to very different ideas on what it is that goes wrong with him.

One of the main goals of abnormal psychology is the classification of various "psychopathological conditions" or mental disorders.[1] Yet it is precisely in this area where some of the greatest conflict is found, and where a controversial issue arises:

What are mental disorders?

---

[1] Many terms have been used to refer to psychological abnormalities (e.g., crazy, insane, nervous breakdown, sick, disturbed, lunatic, mad). All of these refer to similar phenomena (with the exception of "insane" which has a primarily legal application). Although no term is completely neutral, we will use the term "mental disorder" as though it were neutral, referring to abnormal functioning which may include abnormal thought or behavior, or both.

Did the young man in my office suffer from a "mental illness," a "behavior disorder," a "problem with sin," "demon possession," or some combination of these?

Although very few secular psychologists would be concerned with sin or demon possession, all psychologists working in the area of abnormal psychology must deal with the "mental illness" vs "behavior disorder" issue. Thus, once again we are dealing with an issue which is controversial not only for Christians but also for non-Christians.

MENTAL ILLNESS

Hippocrates, the father of modern medicine, was probably the first to suggest that mental disorders were illnesses. He prescribed rest in peaceful surroundings for the afflicted. Contemporary medicine has continued to claim mental disorders as its province.

In this view mental illnesses are assumed to be similar to other illnesses. Each type of disorder is believed to have a particular pattern of onset, treatment, and recovery. The primary purpose of the area of abnormal psychology is seen as the discovery of the common symptoms for each type of disorder so that accurate diagnosis may be made and correct treatment prescribed.

In this "medical model" it is assumed that psychological symptoms are a sign of either complex psychological or physiological disturbances. Symptoms can only be alleviated by dealing with the underlying cause: to deal only with the symptom would be to complicate the problem. Physical "therapies" may include drugs, electro-convulsive shock therapy (ECT), or psychosurgery. The preferred form of non-physical therapy in the medical model is some form of psychoanalysis.

Also assumed in a medical model is a "doctor-patient" relationship. This tends to place the patient in a subservient role vis-a-vis the doctor, who it is hoped will have the tools necessary to cure the patient. Most practitioners will not accept this responsibility, although it is frequently an

149

initial expectation of their patients. It was at least partially this placement of responsibility onto the doctor in the doctor-patient relationship which has prompted Carl Rogers and others to redefine the relationship in non-medical terms (e.g., "therapist-client").

The most widely used classification system for mental disorders is based on the medical model. It is called the "Diagnostic and Statistical Manual of Mental Disorders." The third edition (DSM-III) was published by the American Psychiatric Association in 1980.

From this viewpoint the young man in my office would probably be diagnosed after a medical examination, a case history, and interview, and possibly the administration of some psychological tests, as having a mental illness, possibly schizophrenia.[1] This disease, most of whose victims are young people, is characterized by irrational thought, withdrawal, and often inappropriate emotion. On the basis of factors such as the young man's health, the amount of stress in his environment, and the period of onset, a treatment would be prescribed, and a prognosis given (predicted chance of recovery).

BEHAVIOR DISORDER

Many psychologists and psychiatrists are not happy with the medical model of psychological disturbance. They believe that assuming an underlying cause for a disorder complicates the matter needlessly. They prefer to focus on the actual problem thought and behavior rather than assuming a hidden cause. They would say that the symptom is the disorder. If we get rid of the symptoms, we have cured the problem.

The "mental illness" approach has also been criticized because it may encourage, unintentionally, a dependency of the "patient" upon

---

[1]   The word schizophrenia is derived from Latin words meaning "splitting of the mind." The split referred to is between the individual and reality. It is not to be confused with the "dissociative reaction" commonly known as "split (or multiple) personality."

150

the "doctor," which allows the patient to avoid responsibility for his or her problems. The patient may feel that if their mental illness is truly an illness then he or she is no more responsible for its cure than if the illness were cancer.

Critics of the medical model also point out the dangers of a labelling system such as DSM-III, which is often associated with this approach. Labels have a way of short-circuiting research by conveying the impression that a disorder is understood, when in fact it has only been labelled. ("Why does he act that way? Because he's schizophrenic. How does a schizophrenic act? Like he does.") Labels also have a way of sticking with a person long after they are needed. Finally, the critics point out that there is very little consistency in the application of any classification system, including DSM-III.

If the young man in my office visited a therapist who took a non-medical approach, he would find the therapist not particularly concerned with classifying his problem, but expecting him to take an active role in the treatment. Noting the obscure nature of any supposed disease, the therapist would focus his or her attention on the symptom(s). He or she would concentrate on the specific thoughts and behaviors which were problematic at the time, implicitly if not explicitly taking the position that "the symptom is the disease."

A SIN PROBLEM

Many Christians are not satisfied with viewing psychological disorders as either illnesses or nothing but thought and behavior problems. They feel that both of these approaches are inadequate because they omit very important moral and spiritual questions. Consequently, the important issue of moral responsibility is not dealt with adequately.

They feel that since humanity's most basic problem is alienation from God as a result of sin, no other difficulty can be dealt with until the relationship with God has been restored. Thus the first goal of therapy is to bring the client to the place of acknowledging his or her need, and asking

151

for divine forgiveness through Jesus Christ. Once the client has placed his or her trust in God, and is operating within the same religious conceptual framework as the therapist, therapy can then proceed to the identification of specific disturbances of thought and behavior. These are seen as examples of sin in that the individual is either acting in a sinful way towards others, or is harbouring sinful thoughts and attitudes within. The therapist will assist the individual to identify, confess, and forsake these sins. The goal of therapy is seen primarily in terms of spiritual growth and a "closer walk with God."[1]

From this perspective the only diagnostic label applied to the young man in my office would be "sinner." His primary need would be to commit his life to God. Therapy would be directed first towards bringing him to an awareness of his need, second towards confronting him with his sinful thoughts, and then third, instructing him in right living.

DEMON POSSESSION

The oldest explanation for abnormal thought and behavior is demon possession. Ancient cave-drawings depict holes being made in the skulls of disturbed individuals presumably to allow the escape of evil spirits. Demon possession is mentioned in the New Testament, particularly the Gospels, and was the favorite explanation for all abnormal behavior up until the rise of modern psychology in the last 150 years.

Contemporary psychology has largely discredited the excesses of the past, to the extent that many Christians believe the references to demon possession in the Bible were merely a primitive description of mental illness (on a par with the term "lunatic" or "moon-crazed").

On the other hand, many other Christians accept the Gospel record as well as the many missionary accounts, as accurate evidence of a very real and

---

[1] See our discussion of the "Bible only" approach to therapy in chapter 9.

contemporary phenomenon.[1] They are more inclined to consider all mental disorders as demon possession rather than the reverse. This position is refined by some to include degrees of demonic influence from oppression to possession, the common thread being their demonic source.[2]

Although the demon possession explanation of mental disorders declined with the rise of psychology, it has experienced something of a rebirth recently. As some Christians note the increasing popularity of witchcraft and Satanism in contemporary culture they are more inclined to attribute any unusual behavior to occult influence and possession.

From this perspective, the young man in my office was possessed by at least one demon. He would be told by the "therapist" that he was demon possessed. Labelling in this case would consist of an attempt to identify the demon(s). Treatment would follow and would consist of some combination of prayer, fasting, religious ritual, and commands for the demon(s) to leave.

HOLISTIC APPROACH

A holistic approach is a view of the individual as a complex whole of interacting systems. Thus he or she is at once a biological, a psychological, and a social (we might also add spiritual) system; and he or she can only be understood as the unique combination of these (in fact the "combination" is believed to be **more** than the sum of the individual parts). While this approach can be applied to any area of psychology, some Christian therapists have found it particularly helpful in understanding abnormalities.[3]

First, they recognize that physical disturbances, such as brain injury or chemical imbalance in the

---

[1] For some accounts see Nevius ([1894] 1968), and "Demon Experiences: A compilation" (1960).

[2] For a helpful discussion of this topic see Demon possession by J.W. Montgomery (Ed.), especially the article by W. Wilson.

[3] A holistic view of the individual often leads to an eclectic approach to therapy (see Chapter 9).

body, can produce psychological (and/or spiritual) problems. To this extent they accept a medical model of psychopathology. Even those who emphasize sin or demon possession above other causes, would generally check for a physical cause first. Psychological and/or spiritual help may also be needed, but the physical problem is dealt with first. However, seeing the many dimensions of the individual, and the interconnectedness of these, the holistic practitioner would not limit himself to searching for physical causes.

Therefore second, many therapists also observe that some difficulties arise as the simple consequence of faulty learning experiences (e.g., bad habits). Habits (not demons) of lust may so control an individual that the resultant guilt has both psychological and spiritual effects. If this is the case, no in-depth psychoanalysis is called for, but rather re-education or re-training in acceptable patterns of thought and behavior.

Third, some psychological disturbance may be the result of physical and/or mental abuse which the individual has suffered, perhaps years ago. He or she has been sinned against by others. In this case a more in-depth analysis may be called for, perhaps including the exploration of early memories, the recognition and expression of pent-up anger, guilt, and hostility, and inevitably the need to forgive.

Fourth, a holistic Christian therapist recognizes the supreme importance of forgiveness for the individual's own sin through trust in Jesus Christ, and the effect this has on the other aspects of the person. The goal of all Christian therapy, like all Christian development, is "Christ-likeness." Therefore a Christian holistic approach will always include a concern for spiritual rebirth and growth, although this is not necessarily the first issue dealt with.

And finally, many Christian therapists continue to believe in the possibility of demon possession, in certain cases. However, just as it is an error to dismiss biblical and other references to possession as an ignorant view of abnormality, so too it is wrong to view every abnormality as demon possession. Although the Christian therapist

154

taking a holistic approach would be open to the possibility his or her client was demon possessed, he or she would not immediately jump to that conclusion. In fact, experienced Christian therapists usually say the incidences of possession encountered in Western culture are very rare. [1]

Sall (1976) has identified five criteria which distinguish mental disorders from demon possession.

1. Whereas demons want nothing to do with Christ, the mentally disturbed are often very religious, and may want to be close to Christ.
2. Demons have distinct and clear personalities which are shown through the possessed, while the mentally ill personality seems to disintegrate as the individual withdraws from reality.
3. Demons are logical, rational beings; the mentally disturbed are not.
4. Demons converse with others (e.g., Jesus) and thus have "object-reality"; the mentally disordered manufacture hallucinatory voices, and thus have suffered a loss of "object-reality."
5. Demon possession is cured instantaneously, by spiritual means; psychological abnormalities are helped by psychotherapy over an extended period of time.

Thus the task of the holistic practitioner is a complex one. He or she must first determine the primary focus of the problem and then the nature of the treatment(s). In virtually every case a difficulty in one area affects another (e.g. harmful habits may lead to physical and psychological dependency, as well as guilt and moral degeneration). Diagnosis then is not so much a matter of labelling, as it is a case of determining in which area of the life the main difficulty lies.

A holistic Christian therapist would first determine if the young man in my office were suffering from any physical abnormalities (e.g., the effects of hallucinogenic drugs). After this one or more types of psychotherapy might be applied (see our discussion in the next chapter),

---

[1] This position is taken for example, by Adams (1972), Peck (1983), and White, (1982).

always bearing in mind his spiritual needs, and even the possibility of demon possession.

To summarize, psychologists, including Christians, working in the area of abnormal psychology are divided on their view of psychopathology. Is it mental illness, a behavior disorder, a sin problem, demon possession, or some combination of these? Each of these answers has its vehement defenders and its skeptical critics.

DISCUSSION QUESTIONS

The area of abnormal psychology has several other issues which are controversial. We turn now to a brief consideration of some of these.

Who is abnormal? One of the most fundamental tasks for any area of study is to set its own boundaries. For the area of abnormal psychology this means establishing guidelines for determining who is normal and who is abnormal. Yet this has proven to be one of the most difficult problems in the study of abnormal psychology.

While some disorders present unique symptoms and are quite readily identified (e.g., most symptoms of schizophrenia), others seem to be nothing more than an exaggeration of familiar behavior. For example, most people are concerned about their health, dirt, or germs: someone with an exaggerated concern and associated behavior we call an "obsessive-compulsive." Many people feel uncomfortable with snakes: an exaggerated and debilitating fear we call a "phobia." Many people have wondered if somone wasn't trying to hurt them: an exaggerated preoccupation with this thought we call "paranoia." But at what point does a thought or behavior pattern cease to be normal and become exaggerated, excessive, and hence abnormal?

In most areas abnormality is considered to be a (statistically) significant departure from the average (the mean, median, or mode). When applied in the area of abnormal psychology this definition is usually modified to include only those deviations from the average which are **below** normal (i.e., very bright individuals are not

156

usually considered clinically "abnormal"). This means that individuals who experience symptoms such as those listed above **more often than most other people** are more likely to be considered psychologically abnormal.

However, this definition still leaves open two important questions, (a) how often is "more often than most other people"? and (b) what are the patterns of thought or behavior which could possibly be considered symptoms? Is any type of thought or behavior abnormal if it occurs often enough, or if it is considered deviant by the majority of a society? Is paranoia normal if a large part of a society engages in it (e.g., Nazi Germany)? Is Christianity abnormal if the dominant view says so (e.g., U.S.S.R.)?

Homosexuality. The issue of homosexuality is a good example of the difficulty psychologists have in defining abnormality. Until the mid 70's homosexuality was considered a sexual deviance and was classified under "personality disorders" in a category with transvestism, pedophilia, fetishism, and sexual sadism. As cultural attitudes towards homosexuality changed, so too did its clinical status. In 1974 the American Psychiatric Association voted to stop considering homosexuality a disorder unless the individual was unhappy about this orientation. When DSM-III was published in 1980, homosexuality had been removed as a category of deviance. It was considered a problem for treatment only if the patient was unhappy about it. Thomas Szasz, a psychiatrist and outspoken critic of the medical model and DSM-III, has said "...this is as if the American Medical Association should decide that breast cancer is no longer a disease. It's ludicrous."[1]

However, homosexuality is not only an example of the difficulty of defining abnormality, it is also a controversial issue in other ways. For example, do psychologists have an obligation to prevent

---

[1] This remark was made in a televised interview; similar sentiments are expressed in Szasz's books (1961, 1977). For a review of the APA decision see Ferlemann (1974).

homosexuality as well as to cure it?[1]   Is
homosexuality the result of a hormonal imbalance
or is it the consequence of a peculiar upbringing?

Most conservative Christians believe that the
Bible clearly condemns homosexuality.   Thus
homosexuality is not considered normal and the
Christian therapist has an obligation both to
prevent and cure. However, what of the confessed
non-practicing homosexual? What positions in the
Church should be open to an individual who admits
homosexuality is wrong, has abandoned all
homosexual acts, but also confesses to continued
homosexual attraction. Is he different from the
heterosexual who also struggles with adulterous
attractions?

Mental health and the Christian. While most
Christians agree with the psychoanalysts that guilt
is destructive to mental well-being, they also
believe that as those who are "in Christ" "...there
is therefore now no condemnation," or guilt (Rom.
8:1). In addition to being freed from guilt,
Christians also claim, inner peace, satisfaction,
purpose in life, and hope of eternal life.[2] One
might reasonably assume that with all these things
in their favor, Christians would enjoy perfect
mental health.

Yet such is not the case. Christian therapists
and pastors are being overwhelmed by the
psychological problems of fellow believers, until
one is tempted to ask whether Christians are not
less stable mentally than non-believers, as in fact
many skeptical psychologists and psychiatrists
have charged. What is the relationship between
psychological and spiritual health? What are the
psychological benefits of Christianity? Are there
any disadvantages?

In conclusion, the study of abnormal psychology
raises some important questions for Christian and

---

[1] For opposing views on this issue and the question of
the normalcy of homosexuality see Davison (1986)
and Bieber (1986). For a helpful Christian perspective
see Stott (1985).

[2] For a helpful discussion of guilt, including its use and
abuse in Christian circles, see Narramore (1984).

non-Christian alike. The approach one takes to these issues, and ultimately the conclusions one reaches, will depend to a great extent on the basic assumptions one makes on the nature of the person, as discussed earlier. These conclusions in turn will have a direct bearing on the type of therapy prescribed to deal with psychological disorders. Chapter 9 will discuss further some of the issues which must be considered in choosing a therapy.

Finally, Christians studying the area of abnormal psychology need not only to reflect on the issues of abnormality raised here, but also to go beyond this to a positive description of mental health based first upon the example of Christ, and then on a study of the apostles, saints, and other exemplary Christians.

SUGGESTED READINGS

Adams, J.E. 1972. The big umbrella. Philadelphia: Presbyterian and Reformed Publishing Co. Strong criticism of the medical model and traditional secular therapy by a Christian author.

Montgomery, J.W. (Ed.) 1976. Demon possession. Minneapolis: Bethany Fellowship. Responsible discussion of demon influence and possession from several different perspectives. Several good examples.

Sall, M.J. 1976. Demon possession or psychopathology?: A clinical differentiation. Journal of Psychology and Theology, 4, 286-290. Helpful discussion of the problems in identifying possession. Some criteria suggested.

Virkler, H.A., & Virkler, M.B. 1977. Demonic involvement in human life and illness. Journal of Psychology and Theology, 5, 95-102. Good balanced discussion of the role of demonic influence in pathology.

REFERENCES AND OTHER SOURCE

(no author) 1960. Demon experiences: A compilation. Wheaton, IL: Tyndale House.

Adams, J.E. 1972. The big umbrella. Philadelphia: Presbyterian and Reformed Publishing Co.

Bieber, I. 1986. A discussion of "Homosexuality: The ethical challenge." in Rubenstein, J., & Slife, B. (Eds.) Taking sides: Clashing views on controversial psychological issues. (4th ed.). Guilford, CT: Dushkin Publishing Group.

Davison, G.C. 1986. Homosexuality: The ethical challenge. in Rubenstein, J., & Slife, B. (Eds.) Taking sides: Clashing views on controversial psychological issues. (4th ed.). Guilford, CT: Dushkin Publishing Group.

Enroth, R.M., & Jamison, G.E. 1974. The gay church. Grand Rapids: Eerdmans.

Ferlemann, M. 1974. Homosexuality. Menninger Perspective, 5, 24-27.

Montgomery, J.W. 1973. Principalities and powers. Minneapolis: Bethany Fellowship.

Montgomery, J.W., ed. 1976. Demon possession. Minneapolis: Bethany Fellowship.

Narramore, S. B. 1984. No condemnation. Grand Rapids: Zondervan.

Nevius, J.L. [1894] 1968. Demon possession. Grand Rapids, MI: Kregel Publications.

Peck, M.S. 1983. People of the lie: The hope for healing human evil. New York: Simon and Schuster.

Sall, M.J. 1976. Demon possession or psychopathology?: A clinical differentiation. Journal of Psychology and Theology, 4, 286-290.

Stott, J. 1985, November 22. Homosexual Marriage. Christianity Today, 21-28.

Szasz, T.S. 1961. The myth of mental illness: Foundations of a theory of personal conduct. New York: Harper and Row.

Szasz, T.S. 1977. The manufacture of madness. New York: Dell.

Unger, M.F. 1965. Biblical demonology (6th ed.). Wheaton, IL: Scripture Press.

Virkler, H.A., & Virkler, M.B. 1977. Demonic involvement in human life and illness. Journal of Psychology and Theology, 5, 95-102.

White, J. 1982. Masks of melancholy. Downers Grove, IL: InterVarsity Press.

CHAPTER 9: PSYCHOTHERAPY

If you are troubled by unwanted thoughts or undesirable behaviors and emotions; if you decide one day that you are unable to cope with life, or simply that you are more unhappy than others are, or than you think you should be, you may decide to seek help. Although you may turn to family, friends, pastor, or self-help books first, if the problem is serious or if it persists you will probably seek out a professional counselor, psychologist, or psychiatrist. Millions of people in North America seek such help each year. Of these approximately 150,000 will subsequently be admitted to a mental hospital for the first time. Most however, will undergo some sort of "therapy" in the clinic or office of the professional therapist.[1]

Therapy, or "psychotherapy" is a process of people helping people. In therapy a trained professional would try to help you with your problem by using methods and techniques based upon theory and research concerning that problem. Most of these methods and techniques would involve conversation and common helping procedures such as asking questions, making suggestions, and demonstrating alternative behaviors. The difference between the various types of therapy, and between psychotherapy and common sense attempts to help, is in the different theories which determine what is asked, suggested or demonstrated by the therapist.

The many different views of human nature, expressed by psychologists as theories of personality, have given rise to many different forms of psychotherapy. We will consider some of

---

[1]. Individual therapy is used here as the most common form of therapy. However, many problems involve other people, and in these cases therapy may involve the whole group (e.g., a family). "Group therapy" on the other hand, is a form of therapy where each individual has his own difficulties outside of the group and comes to the group in order to be helped (see our discussion under "Further Issues" at the end of the chapter). Finally, it should be noted that many people who do not have problems seek out a therapist in order to facilitate their development. This form of therapy is called "growth therapy."

the major types of therapy and their derivatives.[1] Following this we will consider the controversial relationship between "secular" and "Christian" therapy.

PSYCHOANALYSIS

Psychoanalysis is a form of therapy based upon the theories of Sigmund Freud. A psychoanalyst is a "psychological sleuth" using "clues" from dreams, memories, and behaviors, to try to uncover complex causes for psychological problems which are hidden deep in the unconscious mind. Problems are caused basically by unconscious processes such as conflicts between parts of the personality called the "id," the "ego" and the "superego." These conflicts remain unconscious and therefore unresolved because the Ego and Superego feel threatened by them and block them out of awareness. Thus the process of psychoanalysis involves bringing the unconscious conflicts to awareness so that they can be resolved. Because the source of the conflict is unconscious, and is revealed only in disguised and symbolic ways, the analyst will **interpret** dreams, slips of speech, lapses in memory, as well as more obvious behaviors, in order to gain "insight" into the problem.

During the course of therapy the relationship between the patient and the therapist may become very intense as the patient at times behaves toward the therapist as if the therapist were the patient's father, or mother, or some other significant person in the patient's life (a process called "transference"). Consequently, the exploration of long forgotten memories and emotions may lead to anger, hostility, and bitterness directed toward the therapist. This expression of pent-up emotion produces a cleansing "catharsis" and is an important part of therapy.

---

[1] Space does not permit a thorough investigation of the many forms of therapy here. For more information consult the relevant chapters of a textbook of Introductory Psychology, or textbook on psychotherapy.

Psychoanalysis is a long and therefore costly process usually requiring one or more sessions per week perhaps for several years, rarely less than one year. It is most successful with young, verbal, intelligent, upper, and upper-middle class adults with less severe psychological problems, sometimes called neuroses. It is most often conducted by psychiatrists.

Many of the ideas of psychoanalysis are found in other forms of therapy in modified form. Transactional analysis is a popular form of behavior analysis derived from psychoanalytic theory. The transactional analyst analyzes transactions, or interactions with other people, looking for ways of behaving which represent the "parent," "child," or "adult" within us. The goal of transactional analysis is to teach the individual to interact with others at the "adult" level (this corresponds to the traditional psychoanalyst's goal of increasing ego strength).

BEHAVIOR THERAPY

Behavior therapy is an approach to therapy based upon learning theory. The behavior therapist deals with a psychological problem by treating it as the result of an unfortunate learning experience. The therapist is not particularly concerned to trace the origins of the behavior back to early childhood; he or she is concerned with the way the person is functioning in the present. The goal is to eliminate ("extinguish") the undesirable behavior, frequently by substituting a more desirable one. For example, the undesirable response, fear, may be eliminated by substituting the more desirable response, relaxation, as the dominant response to the previously feared object. In this he or she plays the role of a teacher, with the client being the pupil or learner.

The behavior therapist would consider the client to have a behavior problem and not a mental illness. Behavior therapy is directed towards very specific problem behaviors, such as alcoholism, childish "acting out," lack of assertiveness, or specific fears (phobias). These, and all behaviors, are seen as the result of learning from the social and physical environment. Therapy involves rearranging the environment so that new, more

164

adaptive learning can take place. This often involves instruction, for example in relaxation techniques, and modeling of new skills.

Because of its very direct approach, behavior therapy can be completed in a matter of weeks rather than years. It is most successful with problems which have a clear and obvious focus (e.g., phobias).

COGNITIVE THERAPY

A more recent direct approach to therapy, which is becoming increasingly popular, is "cognitive therapy," or "cognitive behavior therapy" (e.g., Ellis' "Rational-emotive" therapy (1973); Glasser's "Reality" therapy (1965)).[1] The cognitive therapist assumes that inappropriate, and irrational cognitions (beliefs and ways of thinking) are the cause of behavioral problems. "Everyone has to like me," or "I must always be successful," are examples of unrealistic or irrational beliefs. The cognitive therapist attempts to teach the client more adaptive ways of thinking about himself or herself and the environment. This may mean confrontation, analysis, debate, and persuasion.

HUMANISTIC THERAPY

Humanistic therapy is an approach to psychotherapy which assumes that the clients have within themselves the power to grow and overcome their difficulties. The role of the therapist is to provide the best setting for encouraging this growth. In the most popular form of humanistic therapy, Carl Rogers' "client-centered" therapy, the therapist does this by assuming an attitude of complete acceptance. The humanistic therapist believes that clients develop problems when they are not accepted for who they really are, so that they learn to deny their true selves and play out the role which they think is expected of them. In this way many of their true feelings are denied to consciousness, and their self-concept becomes distorted. By providing an atmosphere of complete acceptance ("unconditional positive regard"), it is

---

[1] A cognitive behavioral plan for change was illustrated in Chapter 6.

165

believed that the natural growth processes within the clients will be enabled to overcome the distorting limitations which they have had placed upon them.

In humanistic therapy it is important that the relationship between the client and therapist be characterized by warmth, genuineness and empathy. Therapy generally consists of the client talking about himself or herself, and the therapist conveying a deep empathy and confidence in the client's own ability to grow, by carefully listening and reflecting back to the client what he or she has said. This empathy is not just a kind of superficial acceptance: the therapist must try to lay aside his own frame of reference and perceive the world as the client perceives it. The therapist allows the client to determine the course of individual therapy discussions as well as the overall direction and length of therapy.

The goals of therapy are a more realistic perception of oneself, greater acceptance of self and others, and improved decision making ability. While this type of therapy has been used effectively with all types of neuroses and psychoses, it is particularly popular in attempting to help people without major problems, to grow to their fullest potential.

Gestalt therapy is another form of therapy also classed as humanistic because of its emphasis on individual wholeness, responsibility, and authenticity. In Gestalt therapy the therapist is much more directive than in client-centered therapy, confronting, and interpreting the client's dreams, speech, and behavior. Techniques such as experimenting with different behaviors, and role playing, often in groups, are a frequent component of Gestalt therapy.

ECLECTICISM

Although we have noted the major classes of therapy, there are many variations of these, as well as some not easily categorized. However, most therapists do not follow any **one** particular method. Rather, they take an **eclectic** approach, choosing from a variety of theories, those techniques which they feel most appropriate for a particular client. Although their theoretical orientation may be in a particular direction, they feel free to ignore concepts or techniques they consider irrelevant, and to "borrow" from other approaches. One researcher (Smith, 1982) found the eclectic approach to be approximately four times more popular than the next most widely used method.

Often eclecticism has meant little more than "if it works use it." In an attempt to provide some structure to the eclectic selection process "metatheories" have been proposed. These are simply guidelines for the selection of various therapeutic techniques. Metatheories may be seen as "guided eclecticism."[1]

Each form of therapy claims a degree of success; no one is successful in every case. For this reason therapists adopting an eclectic approach usually assume that each theory has something to offer to certain clients with certain problems, and not to others.

FEATURES IN COMMON

On the other hand, it may be noted that there are some important similarities among the various approaches, which could account for the success of each. That is, it may be their similarities more than their differences which produce positive effects.

1. Each one provides a setting in which the client is important.
2. In each setting the client is free to express himself or herself.
3. The therapist has at least a limited amount of genuine concern for the client.
4. The therapist has training and experience in dealing with people.
5. The client expects to be helped by the therapist.

Particularly significant is the expectation of the client and the genuine concern and years of

---

[1] For a discussion of metatheories see Anderson and Robinson, 1985, Ivey, 1982, and Ward, 1983.

experience of the therapist. All therapeutic settings have these qualities to some extent, and it may be these, more than the theories or specific techniques employed, which are effective.[1]

CONTROVERSIAL ISSUE

Given the variety of therapies available, together with the numerous combinations possible, what type of therapy does a Christian psychologist use? And, to whom should a Christian go for help?

Every major form of therapy was developed by non-Christians. Psychoanalysis as proposed by Freud, and behavior therapy are based upon theories of human nature which ignore if not deny a spiritual dimension. And, while some forms of humanistic theory may allow for "nonmaterial existence," they assume a non-Christian view of the nature of the person (see chapter 7), and none could be called Christian. Thus the Christian psychologist is faced with a problem. Can he or she adapt a non-Christian therapy incorporating biblical principles and a Christian view of the person? If so, which therapy or combination of therapies should be used? Or should he or she avoid all of the traditional therapies because of their non-Christian roots and assumptions and look only to the Bible for answers?

Although there are a host of questions related to the issue of Christian psychotherapy, in order to limit our discussion we will focus on the following question as our "controversial issue":

> Can a Christian be helped by a therapist who uses secular techniques?

---

[1] For research which indicates the relatively greater importance of the characteristics of the therapist see Korchin, 1976; Traux & Mitchell (in Bergin & Garfield, Eds.), 1971, pp. 299-344; Patterson, 1973, pp. 535-536; for a Christian view see Collins, 1980, pp. 120.

Christians desiring to help others have taken different positions on this question. In trying to illuminate this issue we will consider first the position of those who look only to the Bible for answers and who feel that a Christian can be helped by only this kind of therapy. Following this we will discuss the arguments of those who adapt non-Christian therapies, and who would contend that secular therapies even when applied by a non-Christian therapist may at times help a Christian.

Bible only. Several popular Christian authors are known for their emphasis on the Bible, to the exclusion of psychology, as **the** guideline for counseling and therapy (e.g., Adams, Brandt, Hinman, LaHaye). However, probably the best known of these is Jay Adams.[1] In his books "Competent to Counsel" and "The Christian Counselor's Manual" he argues forcefully against the inclusion of any form of secular therapy in counselling. He is also very emphatic in stating that a Christian can only be helped by a "nouthetic counselor" (his term for a Christian, usually a pastor, who follows the biblical methods which he outlines). Let us consider some of the arguments for this approach.

First, no science is "value-free"; this is particularly important in psychology. All psychologists brings to their work certain stated or unstated values which affect the way they perform their work. Psychologists involved in therapy cannot help but influence their clients in the

---

[1] Jay Adams is used here (and elsewhere) as an example of a narrowly biblical approach because of the wide distribution of his books and his acceptance by many conservative pastors. He has also made some of the most strident accusations against non-Christian counseling and even against Christians who admit using secular psychology (e.g., Collins, Dobson, Narramore), although a careful reading of his work reveals (1) an admission of truth in secular systems (1973, p. 76 ff.), (2) use of extra-biblical sources of knowledge himself (1972, p. 44), and (3) an admission that some problems have unknown causes (i.e., not either organically based or biblically defined; 1972, p. 161). His approach is also similar to Mowrer's Integrity Therapy, although Adams denies any connection.

direction of their own values. If they are not Christians they will hold non-Christian values which, among other things means they will not recognize biblical authority, they will not recognize the existence of sin, and in therapy they will not confront sin (the basic cause of all disorders).

Second, each of the major secular forms of therapy has a "fatal flaw" which renders it unusable to the Christian therapist (Adams, 1973, p. 76 ff.). Psychoanalysis views the individual as controlled by instincts and unconscious conflicts and therefore not responsible for what he or she does. Behaviorism rejects biblical authority and sees humans as animals to be manipulated. Humanism assumes the person is good, and autonomous, and therefore doesn't need God, the Bible, or others. Thus every secular approach is clearly at odds with basic Christian beliefs.

Third, God in His wisdom, has included in the Bible all of the answers to every problem the counselor may face. Since all of our difficulties arise from our fallen sinful nature, that is, their root cause is sin, it follows that the path to wholeness lies in confession and right living. The role of the therapist is to discover the underlying sin in the client's life and confront the client with it, clearly and firmly. When the sin has been confessed and forsaken the therapist instructs the client in biblical right living. Initially, therapy will usually involve confrontation as the source of the problem is dealt with. Later, continued health and development will be assured through instruction and guidance in spiritual growth. [1]

In this view there is no role for secular therapy. As Adams says, "There is, therefore, no place in a biblical scheme for the psychiatrist as a separate practitioner" (1973, p. 9). Therefore, when we ask, "Can a Christian be helped by a therapist who uses secular techniques?" this position responds with an emphatic "No!" All effective therapy is accomplished by Christians, and a Christian has no

---

[1] The therapist is usually a minister since all ministers are competent by virtue of their biblical training, and all persons with a life-calling to counseling should become ministers (1973, p. 12)).

170

business going to anyone but another qualified Christian (i.e., a minister), for help.

Christian eclecticism. In contrast to this "Bible only" position, many other Christians make extensive use of secular therapies, adding Christian values and a biblical view of the person (e.g., Collins, Crabb, Narramore, Tournier). There are several "justifications" which may be noted for this "Christian eclecticism."

First, and probably foremost, is the basic assumption that Scripture, reliable as it is, is not an exhaustive source of knowledge, and that science, including psychology, is also a valuable means of learning about creation. This means that valid truths may be discovered by secular researchers, and be contained in secular theories, although these will always be incomplete as long as revealed truth is excluded. Therefore a combination is the most complete source of helpful knowledge. However, it is most important to note that this "combination" must embody true integration; that is, it must be a careful development from biblically established assumptions on the nature of the person. To merely "tack on" Scripture verses to secular techniques is to create what Crabb (1977) calls a "tossed salad," and is not only unworthy of the name "Christian," but also very dangerous.

Second, some Christians follow Viktor Frankl in making a clear distinction between therapy and religion: "...the goal of psychotherapy is to heal the soul, to make it healthy; the aim of religion is something essentially different--to save the soul" (1955, p. xiv). Since the goals of therapy and religion are different, the therapist (secular or Christian) may perform a valuable service without necessarily becoming involved in "religious" matters.

Third, this distinction may be extended to include a view of the person which sees the different practitioners operating on different "parts" of the individual (body, mind, spirit). Just as the physician deals with the body without necessarily involving the spirit,· so too the psychologist can deal with the mind without always including the spirit. Although physicians will be

171

more effective if in their treatment they incorporate prayer and inspire faith, they will not be ineffective if they do not; similarly with psychotherapists. Although some problems which therapists (and physicians) encounter will have spiritual causes (e.g., guilt), and can be effectively dealt with only by spiritually aware helpers (physicians or therapists), still other problems may have purely natural, even physical causes, and may receive help from knowledgeable secular sources.

Obviously this means the most effective helper will be one who is sensitive to needs in more than one area (e.g., the Christian psychotherapist). But it does not rule out the possibility of some aid from a helper whose view is limited. As Gary Collins says of Christian psychologist Paul Tournier, "...Tournier believes that all healing comes from God, who may choose to work through a believer but who also works through atheists" (1973, p. 121). Thus secular theories and even secular therapists may be useful to Christians and "Christian eclectics" would answer our "controversial issue" with a qualified "Yes." Christians may be helped by a therapist using secular techniques, particularly if that therapist is a Christian who has adapted his or her therapy to Christian values and a biblical view of the person. Nevertheless, even a non-Christian therapist may, by the grace of God, be of some help to a Christian.[1]

In summary, Christian therapists, and those seeking help from Christian therapists, must decide what role, if any, secular therapy can play in the treatment they give and receive. On the one hand are those who hold that the Bible is the **only** reliable guide to counseling and therapy, and that it does not need to be "rounded out" by secular psychology. On the other hand are those equally sincere Christians who "add to" their biblical

---

[1] Another side to this coin is the question of non-professional sources of help (e.g., paraprofessionals and friends). Is an advanced degree necessary? For further information see Durlak, 1979; Goodman, 1972; Kanfer & Goldstein, "Introduction"; Schmidt & Strong, 1970.)

perspective, theories and therapeutic techniques which they consider compatible.

The position which we adopt on this issue is not, as may first appear, primarily based on our view of Scripture. A high view of Scripture as the divinely inspired Word of God may be held by either side. Rather the issue revolves around the view we have of humanity and creation in general. If we see humans as having different "facets," or sides, if not distinct "parts" (e.g., body, mind, spirit), we are more likely to allow for "non-spiritual" help for "non-spiritual" areas. And if we believe that creation as well as Scripture contains truths, both natural and spiritual, we are more likely to accept findings from scientific psychology as well as from theology. Thus, formulating our position on "natural revelation," and clarifying our view of the nature of humanity, as we indicated in earlier chapters, will pay rich dividends as we face further issues in the practical application of psychology in a Christian context.

DISCUSSION QUESTIONS

We have touched on only one problematic issue in the area of Christian counseling and psychotherapy; there are many others. We turn now to a brief introduction to some of these, posing numerous questions for further thought and discussion.

Mental and spiritual health. The fact that some theorists (Gordon Allport, Viktor Frankl, Carl Jung) have recognized the positive contribution of the religious/spiritual dimension to mental health through the provision of meaning and purpose in life, suggests that the converse may also be true. That is, not only may spiritual development contribute to mental development, but mental development may possibly contribute to spiritual development. On the one hand, a religious person finds in his or her religion a "unifying philosophy of life" (Allport), and meaning for existence (Frankl), and therefore greater mental health; while on the other hand, a psychologically mature individual recognizes the many dimensions of his or her existence, including the spiritual dimension, as well as his or her own incompleteness, and is led to reach out to God.

173

These of course are ideal cases. There are many religious people who are not psychologically well; and there are many apparently psychologically well people who are not religious. Nevertheless, our developmental goal, as found in Jesus Christ, is both psychological and spiritual health.

Could psychological growth then lead, through greater self-awareness, to a recognition of spiritual need, and hence ultimately to spiritual development? And is spiritual development hindered by psychological disturbance? The connection between mental and spiritual health needs further study.[1]

Does therapy help? Up to this point we have avoided the question of whether or not therapy, particularly non-physical therapy, actually helps. In a widely cited study, Eysenck (1952, 1961) has reported that the overall rate of improvement for patients given psychoanalytic treatment was only about 44 percent, while the rate of improvement for all other forms was about 64 percent. However, what has proven particularly controversial in Eysenck's study was his finding of a 72 percent improvement rate among patients given no psychological therapy (see also Garfield, 1981; Sloane et al, 1975). This "spontaneous recovery," as it is called, is an important consideration in the evaluation of the effectiveness of any form of therapy. It raises not only the question of the value of therapy, but also the more complex problem of how to define "improvement" or "cure." Therapists from different theoretical orientations use different criteria by which to measure improvement. Is a patient improved when the therapist says so? When the patient says so? When the patient's friends and relatives say so? When the patient has gained insight into his or her problem? When an objective test indicates improvement?

Physical therapies. In our introduction to psychotherapy we discussed the major types of

---

[1] Kelsey (1986) suggests that psychology does not lead to Christianity, although a complete Christianity can lead to a good psychology

174

therapy which might be called "talking therapies." These are attempts to help based primarily upon verbal communication between therapist and client or patient. Another major approach to therapy involves attempts to treat the body, usually the brain, instead of the mind. These "physiological therapies" include the use of drugs, electric shock, and surgery.

Drugs have become widely used in the treatment of mental disorders, and their use is increasing. Drugs have been found which calm hyperactive ("manic") patients, elevate the mood of depressives, prevent the violent mood swings of "manic-depressives," and eliminate or reduce symptoms of other psychological disorders. None of these drugs "cures." They are used to control patients, relieve them of disturbing symptoms, and hopefully, to enable them to benefit from some other form of treatment.

Electro-convulsive therapy (ECT) is a treatment which uses an electric shock to the brain, of sufficient strength to induce unconsciousness and amnesia in the patient. Tranquilizers and muscle relaxants are given beforehand to minimize convulsions, then electrodes are attached to the sides of the head and a brief electric current is passed through the brain. The patient's body convulses slightly, while the patient loses consciousness and feels no pain. When the patient awakes he or she will not remember the treatment or other recent events. Although results are mixed, it has been found that following treatment many patients are less depressed and are more accepting of and responsive to other forms of therapy.

Psycho-surgery is surgery performed on the brain in order to produce psychological effects. The first modern use of psycho-surgery was the "prefrontal lobotomy" developed in the 1930's in an attempt to control violent patients. It involved cutting the connections between certain parts of the brain. It was discontinued in the 1950's because of the unpredictability of the results, and because of the greater effectiveness and reliability of new drugs.

175

Contemporary psycho-surgery has been refined considerably. Its primary use is in the alleviation of severe epileptic symptoms. Malfunctioning portions of the brain are removed after being mapped out while the patient is under local anesthetic and can respond to direct brain stimulation. A more drastic step, taken with only extreme cases, involves cutting the connecting fibres (corpus callosum) between the two halves of the upper brain or cerebral cortex. [1]

Other more experimental surgical techniques involve the destruction of very small areas of the brain. The results of this procedure, although less drastic than the prefrontal lobotomy, are still unpredictable. It is an option explored with only the most severely disturbed.

All of these physiological therapies produce side-effects, some of them permanent. Since the brain cannot regenerate itself, psychosurgery is irreversible; ECT destroys brain cells, producing memory loss, some of which is permanent; virtually all drugs have side-effects besides the dependency produced, and some of these are permanent. [2] Furthermore, the unknown basis of the effects of many of these techniques (e.g., ECT, and some drugs), and the exploratory nature of others (psychosurgery) should make us at least a little skeptical. [3]

What is a Christian attitude toward physiological therapies? The Bible says our bodies are the residence of the Holy Spirit. Body mind and spirit are closely connected in a biblical view of humans (a fact which makes physiological therapies effective in producing psychological results).

---

[1] For a discussion of some of the effects of this operation see chapter 4.

[2] For example, one of the most common classes of antipsychotic drugs, the phenothiazines, can produce a permanent and irreversible muscle disorder, particularly after massive long-term use. This disorder, called tardive dyskinesia, is evidenced by involuntary movements of the face, limbs, and trunk.

[3] A further controversy surrounding the use of physiological therapies, particularly ECT, concerns their forced administration to involuntary patients.

What are the limitations of physiological therapy from a Christian perspective?

Inner healing. Inner healing or the healing of memories is a therapeutic technique which has recently become popular in some Christian circles. It involves directing the individual to prayerfully reflect on his or her past, while asking the Holy Spirit to bring to awareness forgotten memories involving harmful emotions such as anger, bitterness, and hate. The individual is directed to pray with the therapist for the ability to forgive and then forget the wrongs that have been done. Frequently visualization of Jesus, oneself, and others is used to strengthen and clarify the process.

Inner healing is intimately related to the topics of this chapter because of its controversial position in Christian therapy. Some view it as a uniquely biblical helping technique based on scriptural teachings on love and forgiveness. Others see it as a thinly veiled "Christianization" of psychoanalysis, which also emphasizes the need to discover and release long-forgotten emotions. Still others are critical of this and any other use of visualization by Christians.[1]

Is inner healing a Christian or a secular technique? What makes a technique either Christian or secular? (In another example from a different area, is "unconditional positive regard" non-Christian because it is advocated by a humanist (Carl Rogers), while unconditional love is Christian because it is Christ-like? Or does it have more to do with the **basis** for the love or regard?[2]) Must a Christian abandon a technique if it is shown to have a secular parallel or even secular roots?

Group therapy. Over the last 35 years there has been an enormous growth in therapeutic techniques involving groups. Originally developed as a quicker method of training therapists, and

---

[1] For a rather scathing review of this and other forms of Christian psychology see Hunt & McMahon, 1985.
[2] For a helpful discussion of this issue see the article by Robert C. Roberts, 1985.

later as a more efficient method of therapy itself, group therapy became a popular movement of its own in the 60's and 70's. The common emphasis of the group movement on open and free expression of oneself to others within the group was even paralled in the church by a renewed interest in Christian "sharing groups."

Some forms of group therapy, such as Gestalt, which employ role playing and structured interaction, have a long and respectable history. Others, such as "nude therapy," are more suspect. One very popular form of group therapy, est, has been classified as a cult.[1]

What is a Christian attitude to group therapy? What guidelines should a Christian follow in choosing a group? Must it have the Bible as its focus? A Christian leader? A majority of Christian members? The Bible clearly teaches our dependence on one another ("Bear one another's burdens," Gal. 6:2), but where is the fine line which distinguishes Christian "sharing" and sensitivity, from what may be little more than a psychological fad?

Instrumentalism. "Instrumentalism," as opposed to "realism," is an approach to science which emphasizes a clear distinction between observations and theory. While the "realist" assumes that theory is in some sense, however tentative or remote, a description of what actually exists, the "instrumentalist" makes no such assumption. For the "instrumentalist" a theory is nothing more than a "useful fiction." He or she is thus free to use a theory for its practical value, without in any sense believing it. This allows Christians in the natural sciences to make use of

---

[1]   Josh McDowell and Don Stewart devote a chapter to est in their book "Understanding the Cults" (1982, San Bernardino, CA: Here's Life Publishers). A very helpful little booklet entitled "est," by John Weldon (1982), is available from InterVarsity Press, Downers Grove, IL. Werner Erhard, the founder of est, recently announced that est has been succeeded by his new creation "The Forum." The Forum, although superficially changed, is philosophically still est.

the predictions of theories which may contradict the Bible--they use them but don't believe them.[1]

Christian astronomer John Byl (1985) argues that instrumentalism is the best approach for Christians in the natural sciences. Psychology has been heavily influenced by the natural sciences; can psychology adopt this approach too? If Christian psychologists make it very clear that they do not subscribe to the basic assumptions of the theory underlying a particular therapy, would they then be free to make use of the therapy for its practical value (just as a Christian who does not accept an "old earth" view of geology makes use of "old earth" predictions to find oil)? Are not some Christians already doing this when they employ behaviorist techniques (reinforcement, shaping, extinction, etc.) without accepting the basic behaviorist assumption that humans are complex animals, and that their behavior, like all animal behavior, is completely controlled in this way? Instrumentalism could lead to a total "If it works use it" approach. Is this a viable option for Christians? What are the guidelines?

In conclusion the area of psychotherapy contains many very intriguing and difficult questions. Some of these are primarily of concern to Christians ("Can a Christian use, or be helped by, secular therapy?"): others provoke a more general debate ("Is ECT a useful tool?"). Most of them require careful consideration of the basic relationship between psychology and Christianity. All of them are extremely practical and deserve the thoughtful attention of every informed Christian.

SUGGESTED READINGS

Adams, J.E. 1973. The Christian counselor's manual. Grand Rapids: Baker Book House. The author's "nouthetic" approach is developed. The Bible is the only source-book; pastors are the only competent counselors.

---

[1] For a more thorough discussion of instrumentalism in science see Byl, 1985: for an expanded consideration of instrumentalism in psychology see Philipchalk, (Journal of the American Scientific Affiliation, in press).

Crabb, Lawrence J., Jr. 1977. Effective biblical counselling. Grand Rapids, MI: Zondervan. A practical attempt to draw from psychology what is compatible with a conservative interpretation of the Bible. Done from a rational, cognitive perspective.

Collins, G.R., ed. 1980b. Helping people grow: Practical approaches to Christian counseling. Santa Ana, CA: Vision House. Presents a variety of different approaches including Adams, Crabb, Malony, Morris. (See also Collins, 1980a.)

Haule, J.R. 1983. The care of souls: Psychology and religion in anthropological perspective. Journal of Psychology and Theology, 1J, 108-116. Together with the replies on the following pages, this exchange forms an interesting basis for discussion of the relationship of Christianity to psychotherapy.

Koteskey, R.L. 1983. General psychology for Christian counselors. Nashville: Abingdon. Shows how each of the traditional subdivisions of general psychology (e.g., physiology, perception, etc.) has information which is valuable to Christian couselors.

Malony, H.N., ed. 1983. Wholeness and holiness. Grand Rapids: Baker. Twenty-three articles on the relationship between Christian faith and psychology (primarily applied psychology).

REFERENCES AND OTHER SOURCES

Adams, J.E. 1971. Competent to counsel. Grand Rapids: Baker Book House.

Adams, J.E. 1972. The big umbrella. Philadelphia: Presbyterian and Reformed Publishing Co.

Adams, J.E. 1973. The Christian counselor's manual. Grand Rapids: Baker Book House.

Anderson, T., & Robinson, E. 1985. The developmental change agent: A style-shift approach to human development. Unpublished paper, Trinity Western University.

Byl, J. 1985, March. Instrumentalism: A third option. Journal of the American Scientific Affiliation, 11-18.

Collins, G.R. 1973. The_Christian_psychology_of Paul_Tournier. Grand Rapids, MI: Baker Book House.

Collins, G.R. 1980a. Christian__counseling:__A comprehensive_guide. Waco, TX: Word.

Collins, G.R., ed. 1980b. Helping_people_grow: Practical_approaches_to_Christian_counseling. Santa Ana, CA: Vision House.

Crabb, Lawrence J., Jr. 1977. Effective_biblical counselling. Grand Rapids, MI: Zondervan.

Durlak, J.A. 1979. Comparative effectiveness of paraprofessional and professional helpers. Psychological_Bulletin, 86, 80-92.

Ellis, A. 1973. Humanistic__psychotherapy:__The rational-emotive_approach. New York: Julian Press.

Eysenck, H. 1961. The effects of psychotherapy. In Eysenck H., ed., Handbook_of_abnormal psychology, pp. 697-725. New York: Basic Books.

Garfield, S. 1981. Psychotherapy: A 40-year appraisal. American__Psychologist, 36, 174-183.

Glasser, W. 1965. Reality_therapy:_A_new_approach to_pscyhiatry. New York: Harper & Row.

Goodman, G. 1972. Companionship_therapy. San Francisco: Jossey-Bass.

Haule, J.R. 1983. The care of souls: Psychology and religion in anthropological perspective. Journal_of_Psychology_and_Theology, 11, 108-116.

Hunt, D., & McMahon, T.A. 1985. The_seduction of_Christianity. Eugene, OR: Harvest House.

Ivey, A.E. 1982. Counseling and psychotherapy: Toward a new perspective. The__Counseling Psychologist, 9, 83-98.

Kanfer, F.H., & Goldstein, A.P. 1975. Helping people_change. New York: Pergamon.

Korchin, S.J. 1976. Modern_clinical_psychology. New York: Basic Books.

Koteskey, R.L. 1983. General__psychology__for Christian_counselors. Nashville: Abingdon.

Malony, H.N., ed. 1983. Wholeness_and_holiness. Grand Rapids: Baker.

McDonagh, J.M. 1982. Christian__psychology, toward_a_new_synthesis. New York: Crossroad.

McDowell, J., & Stewart, D. 1982. Understanding the_cults. San Bernardino, CA: Here's Life Publishers.

Patterson, C.H. 1973. Theories_of_counseling_and psychotherapy. New York: Harper & Row.

Pietrofesa, J.J., Hoffman, A., & Splete, H.H. 1984. Counseling:_An_introduction. Boston: Houghton Mifflin.

Philipchalk, R.P. Instrumentalism in psychology: Some implications. Journal_of_the_American Scientific_Affiliation, in press.

Pingleton, J.P. 1985. Group counselling in the church: An integrative theoretical and practical analysis. Journal_of_Psychology_and Theology, 13, 21-28.

Roberts, R.C. 1985, November. Therapy for the saints: Does "empathy" equal Christian love? Christianity_Today, 25-28.

Schmidt, L.D., & Strong, S.R. 1970. Expert and inexpert counselors. Journal_of_Counseling Psychology, 17, 115-118.

Sloane, R., Staples, F., Cristol, A., Yorkston, N., & Whipple, K. 1975. Psychotherapy_vs. behavior_therapy. Cambridge, MA: Harvard University Press.

Smith, D. 1982. Trends in counseling and psychotherapy. American_Psychologist, 37, 802-809.

Tournier, P. 1957. The_meaning_of_persons. London: SCM Press.

Traux, C.B., & Mitchell, K.M. 1971. Research on certain therapist interpersonal skills in relation to process and outcome. in Handbook of_psychotherapy_and_behavior_change. Bergin, A.E., & Garfield, S., (Eds.) New York: Wiley.

Ward, D.E. 1983. The trend toward eclecticism and the development of comprehensive models to guide counseling and psychotherapy. Personnel_and_Guidance_Journal, 61, 154-157.

Weldon, J. 1982. est. Downers Grove, IL: InterVarsity Press.

CHAPTER 10: SOCIAL PSYCHOLOGY

SOCIAL INFLUENCE

CONTROVERSIAL ISSUE
   Conformity
   Compliance
   Obedience

> Should Christians use techniques of influence?

Yes
No
DISCUSSION QUESTIONS
   Influencing Society
   Groupthink

INDIVIDUAL SOCIAL RELATIONS

> Does Christianity improve behavior?

No
Yes
DISCUSSION QUESTIONS
   Sex roles
   Deception

SUGGESTED READINGS
REFERENCES AND OTHER SOURCES

My dear brother Jones,

God has just laid your name upon my heart and I feel led to send you this 'prayer square'. I am also enclosing the testimony of Mr. Smith whom God blessed with a $100,000/year job and two new Cadillacs after he used the 'prayer square'. Follow the directions, and when you have finished send the 'prayer square' back to me so that I can rush it to the next dear soul in need.

Please place your gift on the 'X' on the square when you send it back so that our family can continue to fight to keep this land safe for our children. Thousands of others are standing with you in support of this poor country boy fighting the forces of evil. Remember any gift however small will help.

This fictitious letter, based upon actual appeals I have received, contains several examples of "techniques" of persuasion. Wthout criticizing the writer's motives, a social psychologist could identify examples of "card stacking," "plain folks," "foot-in-the-door," and other effective procedures of persuasion which we will discuss below.

Social psychology studies the way we are persuaded, attracted, impressed, repulsed, helped or hated by other people. In fact, social psychology is concerned with any way in which people influence the thoughts or actions of other people. Although they recognize the role of individual differences, social psychologists emphasize explanations for behavior based on **social situations** more than **personal dispositions**. Whereas psychology focusses on the individual, and sociology focusses on social structures, social psychology focusses on the interaction between these two. Because it is such a broad area, we will divide our discussion of controversial issues into the two sub-areas of "Social Influence" and "Individual Social Relations."

185

SOCIAL INFLUENCE

The study of social influence is the study of the way in which a person or persons causes another person or persons to change their behavior in a certain way. This might mean (a) simply going along with what other people are doing without being asked to ("conformity"), (b) doing what one is asked to do when it is clear one has a choice ("compliance"), or (c) doing what one is told to do when no choice is assumed ("obedience").

CONTROVERSIAL ISSUE

Social psychologists have been able to identify several variables which affect the degree of group influence in different situations. Christians are interested in influencing other people; to accept Christ, to go to church, to support the church and its ministries, to live by scriptural principles. What role should the findings of social psychology play in the Christian's attempts to influence other people? We might state this question concisely as follows:

Should Christians use techniques of influence?

Psychologists studying group influence have examined degrees of influence from mild to extreme. We will consider three levels of influence, conformity, compliance, and obedience, before dealing with the Christian use of these more directly.

Conformity. At the lowest level of social influence people are observed to go along with what other people are doing, often without being asked. Adults are frequently critical of adolescents for conforming to erratic youthful fashions, while they are often just as bound to their own conservative guidelines. Conformity is a common and usually harmless part of everyday life; yet it can lead to complacent and even erroneous judgments. In a classic study of conformity approximately one-third of the subjects gave what

186

they knew to be the wrong answer when four other "subjects" (actually confederates of the experimenter) gave the same wrong answer (Asch, 1952, 1955). Although frequently innocuous, conformity can be harmful when it is inappropriate.

Are Christians abusing the power of conformity when they pre-arrange for volunteers to "go forward" at an altar-call in order to increase the number of non-Christians who will respond? Or are they merely being sensitive to the pressures that the non-Christian feels to conform to those who remain in their seats? Should Christians use this "technique of influence"?

Compliance. Compliance refers to the intermediate level of influence exemplified by the letter which introduced this chapter. Here we have the familiar situation where a request is made of us, but it is assumed that we have a choice; we don't have to comply with the persuasive communication. In the letter we see the use of several techniques which have been found to increase the effectiveness of a persuasive communication:

1. "Card stacking" is the selection of only those examples which support the proponent's argument (Mr Smith's example is presented as if it were typical).

2. The "band wagon" effect gives the impression that many other people are involved, and that everyone is doing it ("thousands of others are standing with you").

3. A "testimonial" is a personal example of the successful application of the proponent's argument (Mr. Smith provides a concrete example of what might be expected).

4. "Plain folks" refers to the association of the person or product with simple ordinary people ("this poor country boy").

5. The "foot-in-the-door" technique is the attempt to get you to comply in a small way, knowing that this greatly increases your chance of complying to a larger request (in our example reading the letter, using the "prayer square," or

187

sending a very small donation are small requests which could be followed up with requests for larger gifts).

6. "Name calling" is a technique which persuades people to reject something which they may know nothing about ("the forces of evil").

7. "Transfer" is the association of a person or product with something that people already feel strongly about ("God," "family," "children").

These and other "techniques" have been shown to greatly increase the effectiveness of a persuasive communication. They are often quite apparent in appeals by religious leaders for financial support. Should Christians use these "techniques of influence"?

Obedience. Obedience refers to the strongest level of social influence, the level at which an order is given and no choice is assumed. For example, we are expected to obey the law; we are not assumed to have a choice.

The study of obedience has proven somewhat unsettling for those with an optimistic view of human nature. Under orders, people have been willing to (a) subdue a helpless protesting individual with electric shock labelled extremely dangerous (Milgram, 1963); (b) administer a drug to a patient at double the recommended dosage, when the drug had not been approved by the hospital, and when, contrary to regulations, the orders were given by an unfamiliar physician over the phone (Hofling, Brotzman, Dalrymple, Graves, and Pierce, 1966), (c) place cute puppies in a restraining harness and give them strong electric shock (Sheridan and King, 1972). However, rather than uncovering a sadistic or evil type of individual, these studies indicate that in the momentum of the situation, and under legitimate authority, people will perform acts which they would otherwise find abhorrent.

The ominous parallel with so-called "war crimes" is clear. Soldiers from many countries and in various wars have committed heinous acts of cruelty and slaughter against innocent men, women, and children. Yet they were not particularly evil or

188

sadistic men; they were simply following orders. The research on obedience raises the chilling possibility that any one of us would do the same thing in the same situation.

The potentially destructive power of religious authority was clearly demonstrated in 1978. In Jonestown, Guyana, more than 900 followers of religious-cult leader Jim Jones obeyed his orders and committed suicide by drinking poison. Christian leaders need to beware of the awesome power of their position, particularly when they claim to speak as the voice of God.

Having identified different levels of influence, and some of the potential abuses of each, let us return to a consideration of the question **"Should Christians use techniques of influence?"**

Yes. Christians are clearly expected to affect their world. We are told to be "salt," "yeast," and "light," metaphors which stress an influence on ones surroundings. Christian leaders challenge us to "Change the World for Christ." The Christian university where I teach aspires to produce "People with an Impact." Moreover, beyond the scriptural admonitions, each of us, Christian or not, has deep within a desire to somehow "make a difference."

Christians have always taken advantage of cultural and scientific developments to spread their influence. Whether it was the printing press, radio, T.V., satellites, or modern transportation, it has been used to further Christian ends. If modern psychology can help us hone our persuasive communication skills, why not? To discard or ignore what is readily available would surely be wasteful. Is there any reason to bumble along in our own way when with the help of a few "techniques" here and there we might double our effectiveness?

Furthermore, the insights of psychology merely enable us to be more sensitive to people's needs. By learning under which conditions an individual is most likely to comply with our request we are able to avoid creating additional resistance, as well as help him or her to overcome existing barriers in their social environment. After all, no

189

one lives in a social vacuum. Everyone we meet is being influenced one way or another; if not by us towards positive Christian goals, then by other forces towards negative ends. It is not a matter of the end justifying the means, (although that argument has some appeal), the means are already in use; it is a matter of wisdom to turn the existing means (or "techniques") to good ends. Therefore, Christians should use whatever "techniques of influence" are available to spread the gospel and build the church of God.

No. There are several considerations which must be raised before psychological techniques of influence are accepted wholesale by Christians. First, it may be more appropriate to think of the influence or impact of Christians as the result rather than the goal of their Christian life. Certainly we have specific commands to do certain things, notably preach the gospel, but we are never held accountable for the results. Perhaps we are sometimes too concerned with where we are going and not concerned enough with how we get there. Techniques place the emphasis on the wrong place. They encourage us to focus on the ends regardless of the means.

Second, conscious attention to psychological techniques of influence is nothing more than manipulation, however lofty the goal. The use of such methods is often transparent and produces disdain and cynicism in observers.

Third, reliance on psychological "tricks" shows a lack of faith in God. Dependence on human ability inhibits the work of the Holy Spirit so that whatever results may appear, do not last. These considerations suggest that Christians would do well to avoid the use of "techniques of influence" discovered by social psychologists.

To summarize, it would appear that there are important considerations on both sides of this issue. The knowledge gained by social psychologists could enable Christians to make others obey, comply with, or conform to their (presumably) biblical wishes more readily. Should this knowledge be used? Is it avoidable? Thoughtful Christians need to weigh carefully their decision whether or not to employ psychological methods of influence.

In addition to our own use of techniques of influence, the study of this area should also make us sensitive to the attempts of others to manipulate us.

Finally, Christians in a hostile world should be encouraged by the consistent finding by researchers on conformity and obedience, that if one person will calmly and firmly resist the group pressure to conform or the authority's orders to obey, a large percentage of others in the group will also stand up for what they know to be right. [1]

DISCUSSION QUESTIONS

Beyond the study of conformity, compliance, and obedience, the area of Social Influence raises several other potentially controversial questions. We turn now to a brief discussion of some of these.

Influencing society. Related to the discussion above is the question, "In what way should Christians influence their society?"

In 1984 I mailed a survey-questionnaire to 1,000 randomly selected Canadians (Philipchalk, 1984, 1986). The purpose of the questionnaire was to determine Canadians' perception of the influence of the church on Canadian society. Respondents were asked to rate the influence of the church in relation to other important groups in society, and to indicate their perception of how the church's influence on society had changed over the last 5, 10, and 20 years. The results indicated that Canadians felt the influence of the church had declined greatly over the last 20 years, and that it was continuing to decline. They ranked it in order of influence below governments, the media, educational institutions, unions, and corporations (in that order), and ahead of only single interest groups.

---

[1]. For a brief, helpful discussion of resistance see Brigham (1986). For a thorough review see Maass & Clark (1984).

Particularly relevant for our discussion were the volunteered comments of several respondents who felt that the church should not try to regain lost influence by grasping at the sources of power (e.g., governments and the media), but should exert its influence at a "grassroots level" by helping people in need. Such advice may be closer to James 1:27 ("This is pure and undefiled religion... to visit orphans and widows on their distress, and to keep oneself unstained by the world") than the approach of some church and parachurch groups.

What does it mean to be the "salt of the earth"? How should contemporary Christians influence their society?

Groupthink. Irving Janis (1971, 1982) coined the term "groupthink" to describe the situation in which a highly cohesive group suspends critical thinking and is therefore more likely to make errors in judgment. Because each member in the group values his or her membership highly, and doesn't wish to disturb the apparent agreement among the other members, he or she censors his or her own criticisms and goes along with the consensus, which is usually the position originally suggested by the group leader. The consequence is frequently a unanimous but disastrous decision.

The conditions which foster groupthink exist to a high degree in church settings, making them vulnerable to this type of error. Are the decisions of church boards and congregational meetings **less** astute because group cohesiveness is valued so highly? Should churches take special steps to avoid groupthink?

Under the heading of social influence we have examined some of the ways in which we are influenced by people around us. We turn now to the second major topic of this chapter, individual social relations.

INDIVIDUAL SOCIAL RELATIONS

The study of individual social relations includes the examination of our impressions of other people, our attraction to others, our prejudice and discrimination, and our aggression and altruism towards them. The discussion of each of these areas frequently occupies a chapter or more in textbooks of Social Psychology.[1] Rather than attempt an adequate description at this point, we will introduce relevant material from several of them as we discuss alternative responses to our "controversial issue."

CONTROVERSIAL ISSUE

From the ten commandments to the sermon on the mount, the Christian religion is filled with teaching on right living. One would certainly expect that following this teaching would produce a noticeable difference in the attitudes and behavior of Christians. Thus we pose the question:

Does Christianity improve behavior?

In examining this issue we will discuss the findings of social psychological research which has compared Christians and non-Christians on prejudice, altruism, and cheating in an academic setting. The findings will be treated first from a negative standpoint and then from a positive one.

No. Some of the first research to study the effects of religion (here used interchangeably with "Christianity") investigated its role in prejudice. The consistent finding of this line of study was that the more religious people were, the more prejudiced they were likely to be.[2] Because racial prejudice is so clearly contrary to religious teaching, Gordon Allport called this "Religion's Grand Paradox." In the area of racial prejudice in

---

[1] In addition to the chapters in any introductory text, see textbooks in social psychology such as Myers (1983), or Deaux and Wrightsman (1984).

[2] These findings were reported by Allport and Kramer (1946), Adorno, Frenkel-Brunswik, Levinson, and Sanford (1950), Glock and Stark (1966) and Gorsuch and Aleshire (1974). For a summary and brief discussion see Paloutzian (1983).

193

North America, Christianity did not appear to improve behavior.

The study of altruism or helping behavior also yields some interesting results with regard to the effects of religion. Research has consistently found that only a minority of people will stop to help someone who is clearly in need, especially if they are in a hurry themselves. Darley and Batson (1973) found that this was true even for seminary students, and even when they were **on their way to give a talk on the Good Samaritan**. Furthermore, they found that the most "religiously devout" were the least sensitive to the victims needs; when they did offer help, they often forced it on the victim even when he or she insisted on being left alone. Batson and Gray (1981) also found that the religiously devout tended to offer help when it was not wanted. Apparently if religion makes a difference it is not always good.

In another area where religion might be expected to make a positive contribution, cheating, the findings are also somewhat surprising. Using children (Hartshorne and May, 1928) and college students (Goldsen, Rosenberg, Williams, and Suchman, 1960) no difference was found in the amount of cheating between those who were regular church attenders and those who were not. Also studying college students, but employing a more thorough classification of religiousness (Jesus people, moderately religious, nonreligious, and atheist) Smith, Wheeler, and Diener (1975) found no effect of religiousness on amount or extent of cheating, or on willingness to volunteer help for retardates. Once again, religion did not appear to have a positive effect on behavior.

But is this always the case? Could there be other variables which are producing these apparently negative effects? And perhaps there are other situations where religion has clearly positive effects.

Yes. Religion's Grand Paradox was gradually resolved as researchers refined their definition of religious. When the apparently prejudiced church attenders were divided into those for whom religion served a social function and was a means to an end (extrinsic religious orientation) and

194

those for whom religion was an integral part of their lives and an end in itself (intrinsic religious orientation), it was the "extrinsics" who had raised the prejudice scores of the entire group. The "intrinsics" were found to be even less prejudiced than the non-attenders. Apparently an intrinsic religious orientation has a beneficial effect on behavior, at least on racial prejudice (Allport, 1959).

With regard to helping behavior, it should be noted that although only a minority of the seminarians stopped to help, they were all on their way to help the experimenter by giving a talk. Thus it was not a matter of helping or not, but a choice between which to help. If they stopped, they were led to believe, they would be late, and might endanger their ability to be of help to the experimenter.

In another setting, Perry London (1970) found Christian teaching often played a role in the justification given by those who helped hide Jews from the Nazis during World War II. Further research is needed before the role of religiousness in helping behavior can be determined.

Just as the effect of religion on prejudice may be limited to the "intrinsic" orientation, it may play a similar role in affecting cheating. In a replication and extension of the Smith et al. study, Paloutzian and Wilhelm found that among the two religious groups (Jesus people and moderately religious), who admittedly cheated, those with an intrinsic orientation cheated less.

Bock and Warren (1972) found, contrary to their expectations, that extreme religious believers (later defined as intrinsics), were less likely to obey orders in a Milgram type experiment than were religious moderates.

These additional studies suggest that the relationship between religion and moral behavior is not a straight forward one. While simple measures of religiousness sometimes show no effect of religion on behavior, or even a negative one, a more refined analysis often yields different results. Thus the answer to our question, "Does

195

Christianity improve behavior?" is a complex one deserving additional study.[1]

DISCUSSION QUESTIONS

The study of social influences upon behavior is a broad field. It raises several questions which have proven controversial, particularly for Christians. In addition to those already discussed, the following also deserve our attention.

Sex roles. No one living in North America today needs to be reminded that sex roles are the subject of much debate. Most people, Christians included, recognize that there have been abuses which need to be corrected. However, not everyone is comfortable with all of the changes that have been proposed. One proposal which has divided people both within and without the church is the abolition of sex roles through the development of what is called "androgeny."

Advocates of androgeny argue that women are forced to deny their "masculine" traits (e.g., assertiveness, independence), and men their "feminine" traits (e.g., nurturance, sensitivity) purely because of the expectations and roles society has forced upon them. They feel that a person should be free to express whatever emotional style they wish regardless of their sex. For example, a man should not be criticized for crying, any more than a woman is (most North American men probably weep less often than Jesus is reported to have).

What is a Christian attitude to androgeny and sex roles? What does the Bible have to say about the

---

[1] It should be noted that none of these studies was designed to answer the question we have posed. Being essentially correlational, that is, observing whether religiousness and helping are found together, they cannot lead to conclusions about the cause of the observed differences. Strictly speaking, a cause-effect relationship could only be inferred if we took a random sample of people and made half of them religious (an obvious impossibility), and then observed a difference in their helping behavior. Failing this, we observe correlations which suggest but do not prove.

196

differences between the sexes? How much of our present pattern is result of conformity to tradition and how much has a deeper biological or even spiritual basis?[1]

Deception. Most people realize that deception is very common in psychology experiments. This is particularly true in social psychology. In many situations there appears to be no other way to investigate a phenomenon systematically than to employ deception. Thus, for example, people's willingness to help someone in need is usually studied by having a confederate pretend to need help. Obedience is studied by having an accomplice pretend to receive shock and experience pain. Response to stress is studied by leading people to believe that they will be shocked, and so on. Usually, but not always, the deception is explained at the end of the experiment. Sometimes the "explanation" is itself a further deception which is in turn explained even later.

However, as Van Leeuwen (1982) has pointed out this procedure is fraught with dangers, among which is the experimenter's inevitable loss of credibility. Can a Christian researcher in social psychology use deception? If so, what are the guidelines? If not, what are the alternatives?

In conclusion social psychology is a distinct but very broad area in the study of human behavior. As Christians we are called "parts of the body of Christ"; we are told not to be "conformed to the world"; we are commanded to be the "salt of the earth." Each of these statements indicates a different and important social aspect to Christianity. Social psychology is extremely relevant to Christian concerns and its careful, critical study is potentially of great value to Christians. Thoughtful Christians must face

---

[1] For a specifically biblical perspective see Genesis Chapter 2, and De Jong & Wilson (1979). For arguments by psychologists on the value of androgeny see Bem (1975, 1981), Spence & Helmreich (1978), Denmark (1977). For reservations and criticisms see Archer & Lloyd (1985), Locksley & Colten (1979), Pedhazur & Tetenbaum (1979), Bardwick (1973), Gilder (1973).

squarely these and other "controversial issues" and so redeem the field to the glory of God.

SUGGESTED READINGS

Bolt, M., & Myers, D. 1985. The human connection. Downers Grove: InterVarsity Press. An interesting little book illustrating the relevance of various social psychological findings for specifically Christian concerns.

De Jong, P., & Wilson, D. 1979. Husband and wife: The sexes in Scripture and society. Grand Rapids: Zondervan. Discussion of the complementarity of roles, citing Scriptural support. Considers the pressure of cultural influence.

Janis, I. 1971, November. Groupthink. Psychology Today, 43-46. Brief introduction to an interesting and potentially valuable concept. (See also Janis, 1982.)

Maass, A., & Clark, R.D., III. 1984. Hidden impact of minorities: Fifteen years of minority influence research. Psychological Bulletin, 95(4), 428-450. Important summary of the findings on the ability of minorities to influence the larger group.

Smith, R.E., Wheeler, G., & Deiner, E. 1975. Faith without works: Jesus people, resistance to temptation, and altruism. Journal of Applied and Social Psychology, 5, 320-330. A good attempt to investigate the relationship between religious beliefs and cheating behavior. Raises some disturbing questions.

REFERENCES AND OTHER SOURCES

Allport, G. 1959. Religion and prejudice. The Crane Review, 2, 1-10.
Archer, J., & Lloyd, B. 1985. Sex and gender. New York: Cambridge.
Asch, S.E. 1952. Social psychology. Englewood Cliffs, N.J.: Prentice-Hall.
Asch, S.E. 1955. Opinions and social pressures. Scientific American, 193, 31-35.

Bardwick, J.M. 1973. Women's liberation: Nice idea, but it won't be easy. Psychology Today, 6(12), 26-33, 110-111.

Batson, C.D., & Gray, R.A. 1981. Religious orientation and helping behavior: Responding to one's own or the victim's needs? Journal of Personality and Social Psychology, 40, 511-520.

Bem, S.L. 1975. Androgeny vs. the tight little lives of fluffy women and chesty men. Psychology Today, 9(4), 58-62.

Bem, S.L. 1981. Gender schema theory: A cognitive account of sex typing. Psychological Review, 88, 354-364.

Bock, D.C., & Warren, N.C. 1972. Religious belief as a factor in obedience to destructive commands. Review of Religious Research, 13, 185-191.

Bolt, M. & Myers, D. 1985. The human connection. Downers Grove: InterVarsity Press.

Brigham, J.C. 1986. Social psychology. Boston: Little, Brown & Company.

Cook, E.P. 1985. Psychological androgeny. New York: Pergamon Press.

Darley, J.M., & Batson, C.D. 1973. From Jerusalem to Jericho: A study of situational and dispositional variables in helping behavior. Journal of Personal and Social Psychology, 27, 100-108.

Deaux, K., & Wrightsman, L.S. 1984. Social psychology in the 80s. (4th ed.). Monterey, CA: Brooks/Cole.

De Jong, P., & Wilson, D. 1979. Husband and wife: The sexes in Scripture and society. Grand Rapids: Zondervan.

Denmark, F.L. 1977. The psychology of women: An overview of an emerging field. Personality and Social Psychology Bulletin, 3, 356-367.

Gilder, G.F. 1973. Sexual suicide. New York: Quadrangle Books.

Goldsen, R., Rosenberg, M., Williams, R.M., & Suchman, E.A. What college students think. New York: Van Nostrand.

Hartshorne, H., & May, M.A. 1928. Studies in deceit. New York: Macmillan.

Hofling, C.K., Brotzman, E., Dalrymple, S., Graves, N., & Pierce, C.M. 1966. An experimental study in nurse-physician relationships. Journal of Nervous and Mental Disease, 143, 171-180.

Janis, I. 1971, November. Groupthink. Psychology Today, 43-46.

Janis, I 1982. Victims of groupthink. Boston: Houghton Mifflin.

Locksley, A., & Colten, M.E. 1979. Psychological androgeny: A case of mistaken identity? Journal of Personality and Social Psychology, 37, 1017-1031.

London, P. 1970. The rescuers: Motivational hypotheses about Christians who saved Jews from the Nazis. In Macauley, J., & Berkowitz, L. (Eds.), Altruism and helping behavior. New York: Academic Press.

Maass, A., & Clark, R.D., III. 1984. Hidden impact of minorities: Fifteen years of minority influence research. Psychological Bulletin, 95(4), 428-450.

Myers, D.G. 1987. Social psychology, (2nd ed.). New York: McGraw-Hill.

Milgram, S. 1963. Behavioral study of obedience. Journal of Abnormal and Social Psychology, 67, 371-378.

Paloutzian, R.F., & Wilhelm, R. 1983, August. Faith and works? A behavioral study of religion, cheating, and altruism. Paper presented at the meeting of the American Psychological Association, Anaheim, CA.

Pedhazur, E.J., & Tetenbaum, T.J. 1979. Bem sex-role inventory: A theoretical and methodological critique. Journal of Personality and Social Psychology, 37, 996-1017

Philipchalk, R.P. 1984. The impact of the church on Canadian society. Paper presented to the National Christian Education Study Seminar, June, Toronto, Canada.

Philipchalk, R.P. 1986. Church increasingly influential in society. Catholic New Times, 10, 8.

Sheridan, C.L., & King, R.G. 1972. Obedience to authority with an authentic victim. Proceedings of the 80th Annual Convention, American Psychological Association, Part I, 7, 165-166.

Smith, R.E., Wheeler, G., & Diener, E. 1975. Faith without works: Jesus people, resistance to temptation, and altruism. Journal of Applied Social Psychology, 5, 320-330.

Spence, J., & Helmreich, R. 1978. Masculinity and feminity. Austin: University of Texas Press.

Spilka, B., & Loffredo, L. 1982, April. Classroom cheating among religious students: Some factors affecting perspectives, actions, and justifications. Paper presented at the 1982 convention of the Rocky Mountain Psychological Association, Albuquerque, New Mexico.

VanLeeuwen, M.S. 1982. The sorcerer's apprentice: A Christian looks at the changing face of psychology. Downers Grove, IL: InterVarsity Press.

CHAPTER 11: CONCLUSION

BASIS FOR RELATING PSYCHOLOGY AND CHRISTIANITY

SUGGESTED READINGS

REFERENCES AND OTHER SOURCES

In the preceding chapters we have examined each of the major sub-areas of psychology from a Christian perspective. This has taken us into several areas not often considered in books on psychology and Christianity. While most authors consider the relationship between these two areas as it relates to personality theory, counselling, and psychotherapy, we have explored issues in every major field of contemporary psychology, from physiological psychology to social psychology.

In each area we have pointed out several potentially "controversial issues." Some of these were merely identified, with little or no discussion, while others were examined in greater detail. These discussions were not intended to provide definitive answers to the issues raised but rather to be illustrative of a process of open enquiry based upon Christian assumptions.

It is my belief that the relating of psychology and Christianity is one of the most important intellectual challenges facing contemporary Christians. If Christianity is to be relevant to our culture, it must be relevant to the dominant thought forms of the culture, both academic and popular. There can be no doubt that psychology continues to exert a powerful influence, both academically and popularly, in the western world of the 20th century. One has only to think of the psychoanalytic "man as sexual animal," the behaviorist "man as machine," or the humanist "man of unlimited potential," to see how psychology has molded, and been molded by, the western world view.[1] For their part, secular psychologists are not afraid to discuss Christianity (often unfairly). Christians too must speak out; the relationship between psychology and Christianity cannot be ignored.

Furthermore, Christians have a stake in this field. Psychology, certainly to the extent that it is an attempt to help people, is potentially a valuable aid to specifically Christian goals. The study of psychology may be seen as part of our obedience to

---

[1] For a helpful discussion of world views see James Sire's "The Universe Next Door," published by InterVarsity Press, 1976.

the command to be good stewards of creation. Through greater understanding and appreciation of the processes involved in God's ongoing creative/redemptive purposes we are better able humbly to participate in this work.

It is crucial, then, that we work towards the redemption of this intellectual sphere which has become so influential in the 20th century. It must not be abandoned to the secularists, for it is too important for Christian goals; neither can it be accepted uncritically, for too often its conclusions stem from non-Christian values. Rather, we must filter, sift, and weigh each development in the light of a clear Christian understanding of God and His relationship to His creation.

BASIS FOR RELATING PSYCHOLOGY AND CHRISTIANITY

The foundation upon which our view of psychology and Christianity must rest is our faith in the goodness of God, and more specifically, in the trustworthiness of His revelation. This revelation is most direct and specific in Scripture, which Christians accept as divinely inspired and therefore authoritative. However, as Bolt and Myers point out in their helpful discussion of Social Psychology and Christianity, "Scripture is not an exhaustive revelation of everything that is to be known. Biblical revelation does not provide the content of politics, economics or engineering."[1] The structure has been provided: the details continue to be worked out. Nevertheless, assuming the trustworthiness of God's revelation means recognizing that the "details" of other investigations such as psychology, legitimate as they are, will not in any way contradict the scripturally based "structure" upon which the whole epistemological enterprise rests--all truth is God's truth.

When this fact is grasped fully, the fear of psychology, noted in Chapter 1, is alleviated. Of course this does not mean that we welcome all psychology with open arms, all that passes for

---

[1] Bolt, M. and Myers, D., "The Human Connection," published by InterVarsity Press, 1985, p. 169.

205

psychology is not truth, and we need to know psychology as well as Scripture to recognize this. However, Christians should never be afraid of truth, since they more than anyone else have a basis from which to pursue truth with complete freedom. Unlike secular psychologists', Christians' assumptions are grounded in divine revelation, giving them confidence in the ultimate consistency of their findings.

Recognizing the ultimate security of their position, as well as their human fallibility in interpreting both Scripture and "natural" revelation, Christians investigating psychology must show (a) a willingness to explore difficult issues, (b) an ability to suspend judgment, and (c) an openness to the unexpected. In so doing they can avoid the twin errors of naive acceptance of every claim (e.g., unconscious mind control), and premature rejection of apparently unacceptable views (e.g., Christian hypnosis), while remaining true to their basic Christian commitment. In this, as in so many other areas, truth seems to lie between extremes, and the easy answer is usually found to be unsatisfactory.

We are challenged to redeem psychology through the development of a thoroughly Christian perspective which rests solidly upon explicitly Biblical assumptions. This urgent task can only be accomplished as we face squarely the "controversial issues" in every realm of the discipline.

SUGGESTED READINGS

Lewis, C.S. [1948] 1984. Fernseeds and elephants. London: Fontana. An excellent volume of essays which contains the inspiring and challenging "On learning in wartime." This essay is a justification for learning when other things (war, the end of the age) may seem more pressing. It is also an inspiring challenge to Christians in every academic field to see their work as a calling ("the learned life then is, for some, a duty").

The several books on integration noted in the "References and Other Sources" following Chapter 1, are also relevant here.

206

Although other psychology journals deal with religious issues (e.g., Journal of Pastoral Psychology, Journal for the Scientific Study of Religion) the following ones deal more explicitly with the relationship between psychology and Christianity and so are recommended here.

Journal of the American Scientific Affiliation. P.O. Box. J, Ipswich, MA 01938. Represents conservative Christian views from a broad spectrum of the sciences, including psychology--primarily of a theoretical nature. Includes book reviews.

Journal of Psychology and Christianity. CAPS International, 26705 Farmington Road, Farmington Hills, MI 48018. Represents Christian psychologists working in a variety of settings, from academic to pastoral. Emphasis on counseling and applied concerns. Includes book reviews.

Journal of Psychology and Theology. Rosemead School of Psychology, school of Biola University, 13800 Biola Ave., La Mirada, CA 90639. Strong emphasis on integration of theology and psychology. Although many views are represented, this is a good source for Christian views of psychoanalysis. Includes book reviews.

REFERENCES AND OTHER SOURCES

Bolt, M. & Myers, D. 1985. The human connection. Downers Grove: InterVarsity Press.
Burrows, R.J.L. 1986, May. Americans get religion in the new age: Anything is permissable if everything is God. Christianity Today, pp. 17-23.
Cosgrove, M. 1982. B.F. Skinner's behaviorism: An analysis. Grand Rapids: Zondervan.
Groothuis, D.R. 1986. Unmasking the New Age. Downers Grove, IL: InterVarsity Press.
Kilpatrick, W. 1985. The emperor's new clothes: The naked truth about psychology. Crossway Books.
Lewis, C.S. [1948] 1984. Fernseeds and elephants. London: Fontana.

Schaeffer, F. 1972. Back_to_freedom_and_dignity. Downers Grove: InterVarsity Press.
Sire, J. 1976. The_universe_next_door. Downers Grove: InterVarsity Press.
Tart, C.T., ed. 1975. Transpersonal_psychology. New York: Harper & Row.

Index of Names

Wrightsman 199
Wundt 15

Yorkston 182

Ziegler 66, 81, 144

Index of Subjects

214

215

217